D1628014

Graphic Design in Urban Environments

WITHDRAWN
LIVERPOOL JMU LIBRARY
3 1111 01498 3249

Graphic Design in Urban Environments

ROBERT HARLAND

Bloomsbury Academic
An imprint of Bloomsbury Publishing Plc

B L O O M S B U R Y
LONDON • OXFORD • NEW YORK • NEW DELHI • SYDNEY

Bloomsbury Academic

An imprint of Bloomsbury Publishing Plc

50 Bedford Square	1385 Broadway
London	New York
WC1B 3DP	NY 10018
UK	USA

www.bloomsbury.com

BLOOMSBURY and the Diana logo are trademarks of Bloomsbury Publishing Plc

First published 2016

© Robert Harland, 2016

Robert Harland has asserted his right under the Copyright, Designs and Patents Act, 1988,
to be identified as Author of this work.

All rights reserved. No part of this publication may be reproduced or transmitted
in any form or by any means, electronic or mechanical, including photocopying, recording,
or any information storage or retrieval system, without prior permission in writing
from the publishers.

No responsibility for loss caused to any individual or organization acting on
or refraining from action as a result of the material in this publication can be
accepted by Bloomsbury or the author.

British Library Cataloguing-in-Publication Data
A catalogue record for this book is available from the British Library.

ISBN:	HB:	978-1-4725-9775-5
	PB:	978-1-4725-9774-8
	ePDF:	978-1-4725-9777-9
	ePub:	978-1-4725-9776-2

Library of Congress Cataloging-in-Publication Data
A catalog record for this book is available from the Library of Congress.

Cover design: Louise Dugdale
Cover image: Queen Elizabeth Olympic Park, London, UK (2015). © Robert Harland
Typeset by RefineCatch Limited, Bungay, Suffolk
Printed and bound in India

To my parents, who took me to live on the other side of the world.

Contents

List of Tables, Figures and Plates

Tables

Figures

Plates

Photographic credit and locations

All photographs by the author. For figure and plate captions read left to right and top to bottom.

Preface

What are the visual communication requirements of a built environment? How do urban places function through graphic objects? Why is this so little understood by built environment professionals? In this book, I explore these questions through the perspective of graphic design as urban design.

By examining a number of historical and theoretical approaches, including those from graphic design historians, urban theorists and semioticians, the book exposes the difficulties with inter-disciplinary discourse about the topic. After outlining the basis of an argument, I analyse this through four key approaches: history, imageability, pattern and representamen. Each of these is supported by empirical case studies that utilize material from a photographic collection I have developed over the past decade.

Through super-imposing a graphic design perspective onto established units of urban design analysis, as well as less formal environments, *Graphic Design in Urban Environments* will look at the way graphic design functions as a layer of urban design, thus contributing to the way cities work.

This book not only fills a gap between the concerns of graphic communication and urban development, it also links the smaller concerns of type design with the larger ambitions of urban design through the inter-relationship of a type–typographic–graphic–urban continuum. In doing so, a framework is offered for thinking about micro–meso–macrographic urban interventions.

There are many who have supported and inspired the ideas presented here, not least the many scholars referred to in the text. I am particularly grateful to those mentioned in the acknowledgements.

Robert Harland

Acknowledgements

This book is the culmination of many influences. I am indebted to those who taught me, notably Chris Timings at Trent Polytechnic, Nottingham where I studied Information Graphics between 1983 and 1986, and Tim Heath at the University of Nottingham where I undertook a part-time PhD in Architecture (Social Sciences) between 2004 and 2010. The title of this book negotiates the relationship between these two formative experiences, and although it disseminates much of the exploratory thinking from my doctoral studies, it stems from early exposure to the relationship between signs and cities (exemplified by Chris's design for the City of Westminster street nameplate) featured in this book.

In between these two educational experiences, and before starting my own practice, I worked in the design consultancy sector as a practising graphic designer where I learned about the systematic rigour required for corporate identity and signage design for large organizations such as Land Rover. For that experience I must thank David Pearce and Amanda Tatham. During my time in professional design practice, and before beginning an academic career, I teamed up with the architects and urban designers Mick Timpson and Sue Manley and learned first-hand how other design professionals functioned when working with municipalities. It was at this interface with local authority clients that questions began to emerge relating to the visual communication requirements of a built environment. This stimulated a move into academia to pursue academic research and has since guided my research interests.

In academia, various colleagues have supported my research interests in a field not blessed with many qualified PhD holders. These included Rob Kettell at the University of Derby and Judith Mottram at Nottingham Trent University and, more recently, Marsha Meskimmon at Loughborough University. In doing their jobs well, they encouraged and allowed me time to cultivate a research agenda. Malcolm Barnard and Marion Arnold also deserve a special mention as colleagues who invited me to divulge many of the ideas in this book as part of a Visual Culture module we taught between 2010 and 2015. Cecilia Maria Loschiavo dos Santos at the University of São Paulo has also been an invaluable collaborator for exploring wider cross-cultural design matters.

The relationship between the key concepts discussed in the book have thus developed over a decade (and more) leading up to publication. Aside from very helpful comments made by reviewers of the book's first manuscript, the content also benefits from urban design scholars who displayed great patience and support in reviewing an earlier journal article that *Graphic Design in Urban Environments* expands. Hence, this book is derived in part from an article published in the *Journal of Urban Design* in July 2015 (© Taylor and Francis, available at: www.tandfonline.com/DOI:10.1080/13574809.2015.1031211).

Finally, on a personal note, my wife Maria and children Gina and Leo deserve a special mention. They have waited for me on numerous occasions when I needed time to take that one last photograph.

1

Introduction

'The streets, the people, the buildings, and the changing scenes do not come already labeled.'

STRAUSS 1961: 12

An everyday occurrence

On Sunday mornings between September and May in England, thousands of parents watch their children play football for one of the 55,000 teams registered with the Football Association. According to the Football Foundation's website (www.footballfoundation.org.uk) a minority of parents are 'aggressive, sarcastic and disrespectful' towards the referee, those running the line, the opposition team and their manager. To curb their enthusiasm, parents are required to stand behind a barrier usually running the length of the pitch about two metres away from the edge of the playing area. This is a temporary structure comprising a dozen or so metre-high plastic pegs or triangular banners hammered into the ground ten metres apart, linked by a strip of bright rope or fabric repeating the word 'Respect' along its length.

The barrier is an example of a product that privileges communication over materiality through graphic affect, meaning the message is more powerful than the physical structure. This book is about such everyday objects that impact on human behaviour in the urban environment. Throughout, these are treated as the products of graphic design in the broad sense: they are graphic interventions in pursuit of improved circumstances in an ensemble of people and place. The aim of this book is to identify the scope, explain the reasons and analyse the impact of graphic design in the urban environment, and to locate it within urban design.

Who is this book for?

This book is written to appeal to the two disciplinary perspectives of graphic and urban design. In higher education, the former is usually associated with art and design, while the latter is allied to the training of built environment professionals such as architecture, landscape architecture, city planning and civil engineering. In bridging the gap between the two, the book will primarily appeal to students of design wanting to accommodate the two perspectives in their work.

Most of the book will appeal to undergraduate students because the intensity of design discipline teaching in graphic design or architecture means that inter-disciplinary thinking in these fields is difficult to fully grasp until postgraduate level. Deviations in the text that consider perspectives from geography, communication studies and philosophy will serve as basic introductions to shared concepts between different disciplines. For example, graphicacy in geography is little known by graphic design teachers and students, yet there is much overlap and complementary knowledge between these fields in areas such as typography.

As the book is about everyday things that we each experience as pedestrians, cyclists, motorists, tourists, commuters, and sport enthusiasts – or any interaction we have with cities – there is a case for the book having wider appeal. In this sense it may be a useful resource for anyone who is conscious of their role in shaping cities. This is a long list: 'politicians in central government and on local councils; civil servants; business people; accountants; engineers; property and estate agents; investors; organisers of arts events and festivals; creators of public art and those who commission it; fire and crime prevention officers; managers of leisure facilities; tour operators; health service planners; education policy makers; transport operators; promoters of economic development; and the members and managers of a wide variety of quangos, statutory organizations, agencies and community groups, politicians, entrepreneurs, policy makers' (Cowan 1997: 16).

Origin, bias and approach

When graphic designers speak of how graphic design is part of the urban fabric the association between graphic design and urban public space stops at the point where more in-depth understanding of the built environment is needed. Extending this acknowledged relationship is a key motivation for this book at a time when urban settlement is at the forefront of human concerns.

Not since the 1950s has a graphic design perspective been so needed. Then, Herbert Spencer pioneered a modernist approach to looking at urban graphics through the environmental photography of the city vernacular with a 'graphic eye' (Poyner 2002: 62). This happened at the dawn of the unprecedented expansion of cities that we are only now beginning to grasp. Despite Spencer's work documenting the visual landscape and haphazard graphic language of the street there have been concentrated partial perspectives emphasizing the graphic landscape, but no comprehensive attempt to integrate a graphic design perspective with an urban design agenda. This book expands on Spencer's work using the same medium of the camera as a documentary device coupled with an open mind about what graphic form in the urban context might be. For example, the squiggle

FIGURE 1.1 *Graphic attributes at the Queen Elizabeth Olympic Park (London, UK, 2015). Both of these 'squiggles' elaborate on the most fundamental of graphic mark making properties in the simple use of line.*

on the front cover of this book that defines the visual appearance of a fountain at London's Queen Elizabeth Olympic Park, and the adjacent ArcelorMittal Orbit sculpture by Anish Kapoor, are both justified in the pages that follow as displaying graphic attributes.

This book also benefits from the author's perspective gained in professional practice during the 1990s through design work on a number of signage and place identity projects, in collaboration with architects and urban designers. At a time when Bristol's Legible City scheme in the UK set wayfinding standards, since copied in other cities such as Liverpool and London, good and not so good examples of graphic design became easier to locate and compare. Poor quality objects in some urban contexts that failed to satisfy basic requirements such as the legibility of letterforms stood out as being sub-standard. For example, Figure 1.2 displays how typography is used to variable effect on two fingerposts, a basic item of street furniture.

Attention to typography is one of the underpinning attributes of this book's structure, which is predisposed towards the relationship between four ascending design fields: type design, typographic design, graphic design and urban design. An association

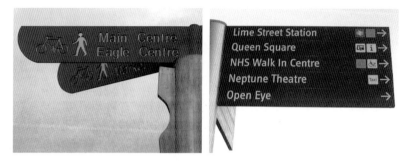

FIGURE 1.2 *Pedestrian signs in Derby (left) and Liverpool (right) (Derby 2014 and Liverpool 2008, UK).*

The recessed white lettering on the Derby fingerpost is partly obscured by shadow compared to the more legible Liverpool scheme.

between them is emphasized to structure the ensuing arguments. Defining each of these in their own right has not been a priority, but understanding the relationship between them has. Particular emphasis has been given to graphic design and expanding on what that may mean beyond its relationship to type and typographic design in the context of urban design. For example, graffiti is one of the most instantaneous ways graphic communication smears the built environment with iconography, but it is neither type nor typographic design. Hence, this book spans four key areas of design practice, as shown in the relationship depicted in Figure 1.3. This positions graphic design as a layer of urban design at an intermediate level between the detailed concerns of type and typographic design (also layers), but within the magnitude of urban design.

A fingerpost sign that incorporates typographic, pictographic and idiographic images into a structure to orientate pedestrians is a relatively simple object. It is therefore surprising why, in the twenty-first century, poor quality examples persist. These examples demonstrate how the design of a typeface, how it is arranged, how it integrates with other graphic devices such as an arrow or a map, contributes to the functioning – or malfunctioning – of a city. This is plain to see (or not, if you are partially sighted). The object-to-object and object-to-space relationship is clear, and should be reinforced by the citing of such things. But the physical scale of type, typographic and graphic design on a fingerpost is comparatively small in the urban context. A more suitably scaled example of the type–typographic–graphic–urban design continuum is exemplified in a project in an English seaside resort. Blackpool's *Comedy Carpet* was created by the artist Gordon Young in collaboration with the graphic design company Why Not Associates. It is a 2,200m² work of art commemorating the town's comedy heritage using more than 160,000 granite letters set in concrete. In this work we see the blend of art and graphic design (this relationship is further explained in Chapter 2) in a £2.6m project within an urban setting, making a significant contribution to Blackpool Council's multi-million pound regeneration of the seafront. See Figure 1.4.

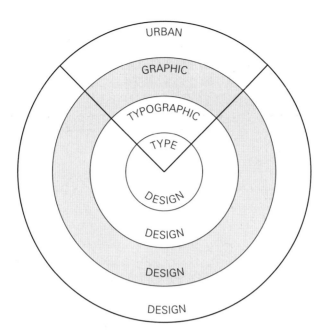

FIGURE 1.3 *Four related design fields that structure the argument.*

Type design, typographic design, graphic design and urban design work in ascending order but graphic design provides an intermediate focus for this book, accommodating both figurative and abstract forms of representation.

The whole project is described and illustrated at www.comedycarpet.com, but the significance of introducing it here is twofold. First, it exemplifies how a graphic object may be judged as a new addition to a town's image, and how it may be interpreted within Lynch's five elements of the city image (see Chapter 4). Second, it portrays the difficulties associated with analysing graphic design in urban environments because when graphic objects are considered as part of an ensemble that includes the urban context, they can seldom be accurately portrayed in a single image. When judged as meaningful interventions in the public realm, as a form of graphic language, the macro and micro aspects are ineffectual. For example, when seen in its entirety, the messages that make Blackpool's Comedy Carpet meaningful as a celebration of comedy are obscured. Similarly, what is embodied in something as simple as an apostrophe is inadequate. The 'celebration of comedy' happens at the intermediate level, or what this book will refer to as the *mesographic* domain (Harland 2015a: 388–389) – see Chapter 4 for more on this. It manifests in the abstract typographic interpretation of spoken language, signature sayings, and figurative visual devices that stand for the identity and meanings associated with comedy. The graphic representation of Dame Edna Everage's catchphrase 'Hello possums!' and her flamboyant eyewear, synthesize

FIGURE 1.4 *The Comedy Carpet (Blackpool, UK, 2015).*

An urban–graphic–typographic–type continuum contributes to the design of this celebration of the town's 'funny' folklore.

at a level that is neither too far or too near to be effective and affective at the same time. The Comedy Carpet provides an empirical example of how we may slice through the domain of urban design to reveal the permeable descending design order of the urban–graphic–typographic–type continuum.

The methods used to develop content for this book reflect the diversity of material that contributes to the notion of graphic design as urban design. Text is descriptive, explanatory, and critical at times, sometimes steeped in historical analysis and occasionally quite frivolous. This is partly because of a desire to overcome disciplinary boundaries and prejudices in preference of a transdisciplinary approach to gain a fuller sense of how everyday objects impact on everyday lives. At times, there is a heavy reliance on the literature due to caution about venturing into unfamiliar territory, whereas other content is more fluent in its appraisal.

Photo-documentation underpins the case study examples that support Chapters 3 to 6. Photographs have been generated under a variety of conditions. On occasion there has been ample time to look at objects from many different positions, returning to look again and again. On other occasions, subject matter has been spotted in a momentary glance from the corner of an eye or in a passing car, requiring an instantaneous response. Parts of some images are therefore obscured or the photograph slanted. Photographs have been included to reflect accurately the moment, the weather conditions, or the sheer fluke of turning a corner and being wowed by the aura of an unexpected object. As noted above, the variable scale of graphic objects that occupy space in the built environment means that it is often difficult to capture its essence in a single photograph. Not only are there inherent characteristics that invite detailed analysis but when contextualized within an urban space, the relationship to other objects may become more important. Objects are often portrayed from many different viewpoints as photographic composites featuring a dozen or so photographs, or many objects feature in a single urban space. This emphasizes the systematic nature of studying graphic design as urban design. To appreciate these in full, when colour is deemed important, they are shown in two colour plate sections. The first section portrays a wide range of situations, whereas the second takes the form of a photo-essay about the white rectangles that form the essence of a road crossing. Such is the ubiquity of this object, its symbolic importance works as both a physical and mental image of the city and civility.

What this book is not about

Although this book will emphasize the relationship between graphic and urban design, and promote the idea of graphic design as urban design, it is not a book about good or bad design. We have already seen in Figure 1.2 that qualitative comparisons are easy to make, but identifying examples of good practice is not the intention overall. There are many social, cultural, economic, environmental, ethical and technological factors that determine whether graphic communication is good or bad. Some objects that feature throughout may be analysed for their respective qualities or failings, but the intention of the book is more to raise critical awareness so that graphic objects may be considered as contributing to the normative intentions of urban design, something Carmona, Heath, Oc and Tanner. (2010: 4) state is to create better urban environments.

Featured examples concentrate on the physical manifestation of graphic elements as part of the city's fabric, not the virtual dimension of urban experience. The physical experience of space may be overlaid with dynamic information accessed through smart phones and other digital devices, influencing human behaviour in what has been referred to as 'augmented space' (Manovich 2006). Amidst a preoccupation with using multiple platforms and the evolving opportunities in environmental and interactive wayfinding, the intention of this book is to emphasize the 'analog context', said to be at the core of human experience (Stolterman and Nelson 2012: 73). For some time now claims that technological interactivity and the 'ubiquitous' nature of 'responsive environments' (Bullivant 2006: 7) increasingly seem far-fetched. The presence of interactive building skins, responsive artworks, intelligent floors and walls, or media installations are exceptions for the majority of people living in urban environments, compared to the everyday street nameplate, house number or pedestrian crossing.

This book is not a comprehensive survey of graphic communication in every street in every city in every country – that is an impossible task. It is more concerned with identification, description, explanation and analysis, than evaluation. A single-authored book is inevitably limited in its coverage, biased in its approach, and contains strengths and weaknesses. The author, therefore, takes full responsibility for the book's shortcomings, but these do not distract from the belief that such a book needed to be written.

Chapter outlines

The book is structured around five keyword chapter headings that frame parts of the inquiry. Chapters 2 and 3 introduce the argument and historical context, and Chapters 4 and 5 align early concerns with longstanding and more recent urban approaches to analysing image and visual elements in urban design. Chapter 6 emphasizes the link between theory and practice.

Chapter 2 concentrates on different aspects of the book's argument. It exposes a range of words and phrases that scholars have used to identify graphic communications as urban objects, and how these do not go far enough to fully comprehend their contribution to the urban environment. Calls from engineers for an art and design perspective on the physical nature of urban systems are shown to be illusive due to the sheer breadth and diversity of the field. Nevertheless, a graphic design perspective is introduced and explained before it is then explored as a spatial practice. This borrows from the established discipline of geography and the way it conceives of space, before introducing Henri Lefebvre's triad of 'spatial practice', 'representations of space', and 'representational space' as a social reality. The chapter closes with another geographic concept and communication competency known as *graphicacy*, with the suggestion that *urban graphicacy* is a useful way to frame the relationship between graphic form and urban context.

Chapter 3 is concerned with *history*. It extends the notion of the urban object by introducing the urban graphic object as a universal communication entity. Furthermore, definitions of urban and urban design are examined, showing these to be broad enough to accommodate a graphic design stance. Putting this study into an historical perspective, graphic design's urban history is reviewed and exposes the role played by graphic objects in the early development of cities in Mesopotamia, and the more refined systems that emerged in Greco-Roman culture when public inscriptions adorned the walls of buildings. One of these forms the first case study in the book. Its influence extends to a further case study of Edward Johnston's 'Underground' typeface, so familiar to Londoners who use the city's public transport network. However, although the Roman alphabet provides the link between ancient times and modern-day graphic design, graphic design history neglects the evolution of urban graphic objects in between. These case studies illustrate how practice accommodates history and recycles ideas as exemplars of their kind. The Trajan's Column inscription and Johnston's underground typeface demonstrate this. The historical coverage reveals that a full history of urban graphic objects is yet to be written. Finally, the influence of design in post-war Britain and an occasional burgeoning interest in environmental systems highlights the massive scale associated with urban graphic communication.

Chapter 4 is inspired by Kevin Lynch's notion of *imageability* and his use of analogy to frame how a city may be read like the page of a book. In this chapter, we consider the city image, its graphic elements and the way 'sign' is a misused and problematic word in this context. Sign is examined in the semiotic sense to distinguish between a label and the object, exemplified by the Empire State Building in New York. Scale is also explored through a macro-micro duality that envelops a mesographic perspective for analysing graphic objects. This framing continuum is taken forward in two featured case studies of urban graphic objects that determine the district element of Lynch's city image. The abundance of graphic images that define the Kabukichō area of Tokyo's Shinjuku Ward is contrasted with the relatively simple design for the City of Westminster street nameplate that not only demarcates a London borough but is also claimed to be 'iconic'.

Chapter 5 is about *pattern*, and also uses urban design theory as its starting point by focusing on what Carmona *et al.* (2010) refer to as the 'visual dimension of urban design'. Although this is shown to give inadequate attention to graphic address, an emphasis on pattern and aesthetics leads onto to Alexander's work on pattern language and the relationship between form and context in an ensemble. This allows us to theorize the Kabukichō and City of Westminster comparison in the previous chapter, and explore the notion of fit and misfit using the example of a McDonald's fascia sign in the historically sensitive Piazza di Spagna area of Rome. Two of Alexander's 253 patterns – the *Road Crossing* and *Ornamentation* – are examined as urban graphic objects in the form of the 'zebra crossing' and distinctive decorative floorscape of Lisbon and São Paulo. The road crossing and ornamentation are adopted as pattern language and the idea of a graphic pattern language is mooted.

Chapter 6 reinterprets the concept of *representamen* from semiotics as object. It substantiates the need for a classification of urban graphic objects but also emphasizes the difficulties associated with this aspiration. This chapter elaborates on the problem identified in Chapter 4 with the way 'sign' has been interpreted from different disciplinary perspectives. In particular, semiotics is shown to be inconclusive and confusing in its use of the word 'sign', and thus, object is discussed as representamen as well as what Kant alludes to as the empirically external object. We wrestle with the duplicity of the semiotic sign and look at how other language use might better work to avoid conflict and misunderstanding. In advance of the final case studies, the function of graphic objects is outlined and then used to analyse three case studies drawn from Jon Lang's typology of urban design as Ghirardelli Square in San Francisco, La Défence at Haut-de-Seine on the outskirts of Paris, and the Theater District and Times Square in New York. The chapter explores how graphic elements are overlaid onto urban design work by knowing and unknowing practitioners, with a final discussion about how graphic objects are used as symbolic resources by São Paulo waste pickers. These examples strengthen the link between theory and practice.

2

Argument

'Every specialized science cuts from the global phenomenon a "field," or "domain," which it illuminates in its own way.'
LEFEBVRE 1970: 48

Introduction

This chapter outlines the argument and the approach taken in the book. It begins by exposing inconsistency in the way urban thinkers write about miscellaneous urban objects be it street furniture, hand drawn graffiti or complete environmental information systems. Rather than introducing and explaining the scope and significance of these individual categories, as others have done, for example under the guise of wayfinding, this chapter contemplates a partial systems approach to how cities work from the subject perspective of graphic design as a selective starting point. It will respond to long-standing calls for an art and design perspective on the physical make up of the city. Finally, and superseding conflicting views about what graphic design is, the chapter argues for graphic design as a spatial practice in order to better contribute to wider concerns about the future of cities.

An array of urban objects

Urban theorists refer to graphic objects inconsistently in their writing. They talk about an array of individual or grouped objects in towns and cities with neither a full appreciation of how variable and extensive these are, or any idea of how to categorize them. Table 2.1 lists the range of generic and specific terminologies used in the literature. Plate 1 typifies a small selection of these.

Lang (2005) groups an assortment of these under 'miscellaneous: individual objects in urban space' and also uses the moniker 'urban objects' to name what are considered as acts of urban design.

TABLE 2.1   A miscellaneous list of urban objects (Harland 2015)

Environmental information systems	Bus/train signs	Notice boards
Visual communication displays	Name signs	Maps
	Traffic and direction signs	Bus placards
Outdoor information media	Systematic signage	Information boards
Architectural communication	Symbolic or written representations	Lifesaving equipment
Commercial vernacular	Inscription	Awnings/sunblinds
	Lettering	Gantries
Public information	Street numbers	Street finders
Public signing and lighting		Bus information
Official, unofficial and illegitimate public messages	Street furniture	Banners
	Flagpoles	Works of art (sculptures, murals)
	Clocks	
	Pedestrian crossings	Nineteenth-century graphics
Signs	Manhole	Large-scale graphic images
Pedestrian signs	Coloured surfaces of a bus lane	Large screens
Secret signs	Painted mural	
Commercial name signs	Wayfinding devices	Urban visual culture
Route signs	Decorative paving	Aesthetic surfaces
Street name plates/ boundary signs	Illuminated traffic bollards	Functionalist façades
		Electric stimulations
		Curiosity objects

Considering the sheer variety of the objects listed, it is timely that we develop a more comprehensive understanding of what they are and do. This is especially important due to the fact that more humans live in urban settlements than in rural settlements. The design of cities is thus a major priority for the twenty-first century. Calls for 'harmonious urbanization' and 'integrated urban policy' (UN-Habitat 2008: iii) confirm that more inclusive approaches are needed. Given the lack of cohesion in the way such graphic communication is understood, seeking a better understanding of how graphic objects contribute to the functioning of urban objects is timely. The economic dimension alone is cause for concern. For example, in 2002, the UK Department for Transport Traffic Signs Regulations and General Directions (TSRGD) withdrew a sign plate indicating no parking 'at any time' that accompanied the use of double yellow lines, to reduce street clutter. Ten thousand of these small signs were withdrawn from the City of Nottingham alone. At the same time, according to Nottingham City Council, the cost of a similar 'Permanent Retroflective Rectangular Traffic Sign (Class 1)' was £70.96. Assuming those signs taken away were installed in batches, perhaps over a period of years, the costs associated suggest that even in a modest city of less than half a million people, significant chunks of taxpayers money are spent on taken-for-granted everyday objects.

Urban design writers lack any framework for viewing these relatively small-scale things, despite the communications function of a city being fundamental (Lang 1994: 171). Urban designers traditionally understand communications to mean transportation, neglecting other forms that contribute to everyday life. It has been interpreted as the development of roads, canals and railways rather than media such as press and broadcasting, and now internet or social media. Consequently, communications has never been approached as an overall system due to the many different agents involved that produce different kinds of communication.

Graphic communication is an urban paradigm, scattered amongst the products of architecture, landscape architecture, city planning, and civil engineering, but not isolated from these established activities. It is part of the urban system, but it has never been incorporated into attempts to understand the city as a whole, as a partial urban system. How can this be done?

Studying partial urban systems

There are as many ways to study cities as there are people living in them. When the city is the subject of academic pursuit, LeGates (2003: 13–19) proposes that scholars have tended to focus on 12 main concerns:

1 The evolution of cities.

2 Urban culture.

3 Urban society.

4 Urban politics and governance.

5 Urban economics, urban public finance and regional science.

6 Urban and metropolitan space and the city systems.

7 Mega cities and global city systems.

8 Technology and cities.

9 Urban planning, urban design, landscape architecture and architecture.

10 Race, ethnic, and gender relations in cities.

11 Urban problems and policy.

12 Urban futurism.

More idiosyncratic perspectives on the city have focused on food (Steel 2009), collage (Rowe and Koetter 1978), iconography (Venturi *et al*. 1977) and image (Lynch

1960; Strauss 1961), to name but a few. From different disciplinary perspectives, whereas the engineer favours a concern for infrastructure (e.g. Ausubel and Herman 1988), for the historian, the city is a theatre, and there is less concern about the technical aspects of road building or sanitary provision and more the city as a 'social institution' (Mumford [1937] 2003: 93). This book adds to this range of viewpoints from the perspective of graphic design. Through that lens, it posits new insights about urban culture, urban and metropolitan space and the city systems (see Chapter 2), the evolution of cities (see Chapter 3), the city image and its elements (see Chapter 4), the visual dimension of urban design (see Chapter 5), and how symbolic resources are deployed in urban planning, landscape architecture, architecture as well as much-less-formal built environments (see Chapter 6).

The opportunity for graphic design to offer new perspectives on established approaches is timely because urban society depends on the kind of symbolic resources that graphic design generates. Furthermore, the increasing complexity of urban environments and the implication for social relations brought about through rapid urbanization has led to the realization that the study of cities requires inter-disciplinary approaches that work towards a holistic understanding of the urban context. These point towards new ways of thinking about the nature of the city and its urban systems that complement, but also contrast with, the established built environment professions such as civil engineers. For instance, even though engineers generally see urban systems as infrastructure in the form of public works such roads, bridges or sewage disposal, they also appeal and advocate for an understanding of urban systems from the perspective of art and design (White 1988x: vi). Amongst other reasons, this book is a direct response to this invitation. Before exploring this, we will briefly consider approaches to the understanding of how cities work and the relevance of a systems approach.

When studying the city, Needham (1977) advocates a systems approach. This accommodates the view that cities work through the interaction between people, places, employers, public institutions and politics, in planned and unplanned, co-ordinated and unco-ordinated scenarios, for better or worse. A systems approach is said to have numerous advantages: one is to study the whole system because it is methodologically more fruitful than partial perspectives; another is that the system is greater than the sum of the component parts; studying the whole reveals similarities with other systems (e.g. biological). Finally, a systems approach also concentrates on parts, rather than the whole, with an emphasis on causal connections. Needham's approach aims to 'teach about *interactions* and *inter-relationships* between urban components and activities' (1977: 2, original italics). This is coupled with two other approaches to understanding the city: 'an ecological approach' and 'the approach of individualism'. An ecological approach is concerned with the 'interactions between the activities of men and the spaces in which the activities take place', whereas the approach of individualism supports a view that people, more so than groups, are emphasized, the former constituting the latter and thus allowing for discussion about 'collectivities' (1977: 4). In sum, these three combine for the analysis of a set of connected parts, the interaction between objects and their environment, and social communication. All are highly relevant to the arguments outlined in this book in that graphic communication facilitates interaction and inter-relationships between people, and their relationship to their built environment in ways that are both collective and individual.

Of these methods, Needham favours a partial system approach because studying the whole system is a 'logical impossibility' in that there must be a selective starting point (1977: 11, citing Popper 1964) defined by the investigator. To encourage a holistic understanding means seeking many perspectives, but these are infinite; a holistic approach realistically means working *towards* the widest possible view of the city from all vantage points. When we look at the relationship between the many forms (all forms) that make up the city, the variation is infinite, thus challenging any panoptic perspective aspirations.

Having identified the approaches taken by urban scholars and implied how this book will contribute to these, art and design has also been introduced as a perspective in need for city discourse. However, art and design is not the selective starting point for constructing the arguments made in this book – that is graphic design. But art and design is where most graphic design is taught, so knowing about it will help to frame much of what will be soon explained as a graphic design perspective on urban environments, and as a partial urban system.

Art and design perspectives

Returning to the engineer's desire for a detailed examination of the city's 'vital systems' from an art and design perspective, White (1988: vi) asks: 'What it is that physically makes up or characterizes a city?' This calls for in-depth consideration from art and design. Responses to this call are problematic because although there may be a general understanding of what art and design is inside and outside education, the phrase stands for a broad set of subjects. For example, the US National Association of Schools of Art and Design 2012–13 handbook identifies 23 different professional baccalaureate degrees (see Table 2.2). Across many institutions, various permutations of these make up the core subjects in art and design departments, schools and colleges; new subject areas continue to emerge.

Words associated with art and design include creative, aesthetic sensibility, intellectual enquiry, team working, diversity, a plurality of research, reflection, and independence. These provide an indication of what qualities graduates possess, but unlike the description of what an engineer does, none directly align to understanding how cities work.

A singular art and design perspective on what makes a city is therefore tricky, despite a long history that dates back to training through medieval guilds of craft

TABLE 2.2   Professional baccalaureate degrees in Art and Design in the USA

• animation	• general fine arts	• photography
• ceramics	• glass	• printmaking
• digital media	• graphic design	• sculpture
• drawing	• illustration	• textile design
• fashion design	• industrial design	• theatre design
• film/video production	• interior design	• weaving/fibres
• general crafts	• jewellery/metals	• woodworking.
• general design	• painting	

artisans in a master–apprentice model of learning since the thirteenth or fourteenth centuries. However, 'art and design is a subject that embraces an overlapping and changing community of many disciplines . . . It also engages with many other subjects, including media and communications; the performing arts; the built environment; information technology and computing; engineering; business; and, notably, the history of art, architecture and design' (QAA 2008: 4). As there are so many subject specialisms in art and design, it is unclear how these can provide a single simple art and design perspective on urban systems.

Breaking the art and design compound does not make the process of understanding any easier. As Landry (2006: 5) points out, 'the art of city-making involves all the arts', privileging the realm of subjectivity and value judgments, sensory experience and complexity, the extra-ordinary above the mundane, culture and distinctiveness. Conversely, design (a word that engineers may more readily associate with) within art and design is most often associated with the conceiving, planning, organization and making of artefacts; obvious examples from the list above are fashion design or textile design. These are easy to identify with as we come into contact with them daily. But design is an expanding notion that encompasses applied creativity, problem solving, learning, evolution, social process, even game playing (Dorst 2003). Newer subject specialisms have emerged, such as interaction design, experience design, or sustainable design, often as hybrid disciplines. For instance, information design combines established fields such as typography and graphic design with linguistics, psychology and applied ergonomics (McDermott 2007: xiii). More than the production of artefacts, design is now associated with services, experiences, environments, and more.

In the broadest sense, design is about intention, invention and alteration, as suggested by the oft-cited '[e]veryone designs who devises courses of action aimed at changing existing situations into preferred ones' (Simon 1996: 111). More recent attempts to characterize design not only to associate it with the designed environment, but also with what Tonkiss (2013: 2) states as the 'complex interaction of socio-economic with spatio-technical processes and practice'. This clearly situates design as much in the realm of social science as the arts, but also illustrates how difficult, or impossible, a singular design perspective is due to the multiple viewpoints within.

An art or design approach is as complex as – if not more difficult than – an art and design perspective, and compared to explanations about what engineers do – they are scientifically trained to contribute to the design and building of products, machines, systems or structures – a working definition for art and design cannot be found in a dictionary. There is no exactness in the way that engineering, architecture, even fashion, are characterized. Rather than try to define *an* art and design perspective, there are, instead, a *number* of art and design perspectives. Thus, the notion of perspective provides a framework for adopting a more focused graphic design standpoint.

Adopting a perspective

We each differ in our perspective on the world. Observations, experiences, reflections, assumptions, beliefs, orientation, culture, habits, expertise, concentration levels, technical competency, organizational skills, personality, disciplinary knowledge, attitudes, and imagination all contribute to our highly individual ways of looking at things. Hence, our ability to compare, contrast and transfer information also varies considerably. Such diversity has led to some closely related 'framing categories' for studying systems. In a discussion about systemics in design, Nelson and Stolterman (2012: 57–91) identify different categories as stance or standpoint, mind-set, mental models, worldview or *weltanschauung*, world approach, point of view, filter, lenses, multiple perspectives and viewpoint. In this book, we adopt a stance, or standpoint, meaning an adopted approach from a changed mind-set for understanding and acting in the world, allowing access to pre-determined schemas (e.g. theories) or the creation of new meanings. Given that there is no singular art and design perspective to frame our thinking about urban systems, attempting to understand the array of graphic communication as a partial urban system will benefit from a graphic design stance. Graphic design can provide this from its position as one of the core subjects in art and design since the middle of the twentieth century, and also as a centuries-old practice dating back to the development of early urban settlements. This standpoint will draw from a graphic design world approach, bringing in points of view, filters, lenses and multiple perspectives that provide a trans-disciplinary viewpoint to unify the phenomena listed in Table 2.1. What, then, might a graphic design stance be?

Towards a graphic design stance

In this section, I will establish what exactly a graphic design stance is in relation to urban design. From a plethora of inadequate and mistaken definitions and explanations, a sense of graphic design as a symbolizing and spatial practice will be introduced as a substitute for the art and design perspective requested by engineers, as noted earlier.

A short description of graphic design reads 'the art and profession of selecting and arranging visual elements – such as typography, images, symbols, and colours – to convey a message to an audience' (Meggs 2014). It is explained as a collaborative discipline whereby writers, photographers and illustrators respectively provide words (verbal) and image (visual) content for the graphic designer to integrate into a whole. The partial nature of this explanation is insufficient to establish a graphic design perspective on urban systems. While satisfying a need for brevity, it lacks precision. Although emphasis is placed on the ability to integrate different activities, a miscellany of visual elements is merely implied. Too much emphasis is placed on assimilation in the pursuit of visual communication, without any qualification of what visual communication might be. The notion of 'visual elements' needs a more precise definition; other tacit qualities need greater acknowledgement. For example, it says nothing about conceptual thinking, one of the defining goals of design that usually precedes planning and making. Greater specificity will come from understanding the recent history of graphic design.

The notion of something called *graphic design* emerged in the early twentieth century through an informal transition from activities associated with commercial art, which was largely illustration based, to something that also synthesized lettering, typography, design and artistic aspiration as graphic art and then graphic design (Shaw 2014). In graphic design history, the origin of the phrase is mistakenly attributed to William Addison Dwiggins ([1922] 1999), who used it in an article for a special graphic arts supplement of the *Boston Evening Transcript* in 1922. Dwiggins, well known as a book and typeface designer, but also experienced in design for advertising, included graphic design in the sentence: 'Advertising design is the only form of graphic design that gets home to everybody.' At this point, graphic design became known as representing a range of graphic practices, known collectively until that point as 'printing art', 'commercial art', 'graphic art' and 'advertising design' (Heller 1999: 14). Dwiggins' intention was to encourage artistic aspiration in design for print. He uses graphic design as an ill-defined concept to convey artistic aspiration in forms of graphic communication to suggest something different from commercial art. According to Shaw (2014), an earlier use of the phrase is attributed to an article about the design of charts and graphs for reinforcing rectangular concrete sections (Poetter 1908) in a publication called *Concrete Age*, suggesting its origins had more rational intentions than the self expressive nature of artistic aspiration.

Over the next few decades, graphic design as a named professional activity became more established within a number of closely related occupations and industries spanning America and Europe. For example, in Europe, professional societies, such as the Association of Swiss Graphic Designers in 1939 (Brockmann 1995: 12) were formed and the professional moniker 'graphic designer' became known in other major

European countries such as Sweden in the 1950s (Bowallius 2002: 2012) and the United Kingdom (UK) in the immediate post-war years. In the UK, it quickly gained high educational status through the establishment of a School of Graphic Design at the Royal College of Art (RCA) in 1948, and a Department of Graphic Design at the Central School of Arts and Crafts (Seago (undated): 63).

However, despite flourishing in America and Europe during the second half of the twentieth century and eventually becoming widely known in the 1980s (Cramsie 2010: 10), definitions of graphic design did not feature in mainstream dictionaries until the end of the century. Barnard (2005: 1–2) notes that, until then, graphic design had gone relatively unnoticed. At that time, the *Oxford Dictionary of English* provided a definition of what graphic design was, reading 'the art or skill of combining text and pictures in advertisements, magazines, or books' (Soanes and Stevenson 2005). Whilst recognising artistic aspiration, this embedded graphic design predominantly in print media despite the onset of screen-based applications in the late 1950s in newer fields such as film and television design. As the profession gained in prominence, attempts were made to capture what it actually was. For instance: 'that creative endeavour which finds expression through the medium of printing ink. It is the design used in the make-up of daily papers, magazines, and books; in display cards, package goods, and advertising literature; and in the reproduced or original prints that adorn our walls' (Friend and Hefter 1935, cited by Shaw 2014).

In the early post-war years, Richard Guyatt – the first Professor of Graphic Design at the Royal College of Art – vaguely suggested it to be 'printing as a vehicle for art' (Lewis and Brinkley 1954: 14). Although clearly an endeavour, such lack of precision matched the difficulty defining the graphic designer's work. For example, in discussions about the profession of graphic design, Guyatt's colleagues cited the work of Edward Bawden, someone known primarily as a painter, but also for his London Transport posters, book illustrations and decorations and more humdrum design for beer labels, wallpaper, press advertising, drawings and decorations for ceramics (1954: 165). Clearly, graphic design practice increasingly stood for something concerned with the visual, encompassing of a range of materials, processes and techniques.

The practice matured over the coming decades and this brought about further attempts to describe it. For example, the *Dictionary of Graphic Design and Designers* defined it as the 'Generic term for the activity of combining typography, illustration, photography and printing for the purposes of persuasion, information or instruction' (Livingston and Livingston 1992: 90). Although similar to previously noted definitions, this elaborated on mere 'text' and 'pictures' to also include a sense of intent, but notably it is still aligned with printing despite the same publication featuring the work of graphic designers doing film title sequences, such as Saul Bass (*The Man with the Golden Arm, Psycho*) and Robert Brownjohn (*Goldfinger*). Furthermore, designers such as Massimo Vignelli, responsible for signage on the New York Subway in 1966 and the Washington Metro in 1968, and Jock Kinneir who designed signage for Gatwick Airport in London in the mid-1950s, feature. With Margaret Calvert, Kinneir went on to design the signage system for British roads, first implemented in 1964.

Others have since offered explanations for what graphic design does. For instance, Hollis suggests its main roles are to 'identify, . . . inform and instruct, . . . present and promote' (2001: 10), expanding on his view that 'Graphic Design is the business of making or choosing marks and arranging them on a surface to convey an idea' (more about the functions of graphic design in Chapter 6). No mention here of printing, but there is recognition of the creative act of mark making, the consideration of alternatives, and organization.

Throughout the late twentieth century there is a lack of consensus on the purpose of graphic design, evident in an explanation by academics who acknowledge a wider (if not full) range of applications through new phrases such as communication media that encompass print and electronic, static and time-based applications (CNAA 1990: 13). They place books alongside computer graphics and video, whilst specialisms that were central to the practice such as illustration, typography and photography are inappropriately framed as technical specialisms. Different intentions are listed as information, persuasion and recreation. Applications include information design, advertising design, corporate identity design, packaging design and publishing design. This broadens the scope of application away from printing to the more generalized communication media, but still offers a restrictive list of formats split between traditional print applications and an emerging screen interface. It also introduces a somewhat restricted group of 'technical specialisms' to define the often highly creative pursuits of illustration, typography and photography. Overlooked is the diversification into other environments such as the public realm, despite the earlier work of Vignelli, or Kinneir/Calvert, and the central role of graphic design allied to architecture in the emerging activity of wayfinding design (Arthur and Passini 1992). Furthermore, and of most significance in these early efforts to formally describe and define graphic design, there is no mention of art – the driving intention of Dwiggins' initial aspiration.

These attempts at clarification illustrate how the idea of graphic design has expanded and adapted to new situations, environments and changing technologies. However, as soon as definitions and descriptions have appeared, they become out-dated or do not adequately cover the full range of activity.

In *What is Graphic Design?* Newark (2002) shuns succinct definitions, explaining that it is a pervasive art. As well as printed matter, Newark acknowledges that graphic designers also design signs, websites, and work in film, using an array of materials beyond paper, from book-cloth to neon tubing, and even boiled leather! In this, graphic design is recognized as a complex nascent activity which is difficult to categorize. Nevertheless, Newark assembles an anatomy of alphabets, typography, images, tools and disciplines, using loosely defined topics (see Table 2.3). Notably, these predate the advent of social media and app design, which now also provide contemporary outlets for graphic design practice.

TABLE 2.3 An 'anatomy' of graphic design

Alphabets	Images	Disciplines
Modules	Illustration	Logos
Typefaces	Photography	Identity
Digital type	Using photography	Print – publicity
Full character set	Word and image	Print – information
Languages		Packaging
	Tools	Books
Typography	Pencil	Magazines
The grid	Materials	Exhibitions
Hierarchy	Paper	Signs
Rules and other devices	Computer	Web and film

In sum, the twentieth century saw graphic design emerge as a compound term for a related set of practices undertaken by individuals and groups. This initially spanned handcraft activities such as calligraphy as well as technical knowledge associated with printing, extending to media as diverse as ceramics, television, film and public signage by the 1960s, then computer-driven technology in the 1980s and, more recently, internet and smart phone-driven solutions.

With regard to the built environment, graphic design is acknowledged as ubiquitous. For example, Lupton (1996: 15), states that '[u]rban public space is a stage for viewing the field of graphic design in its diversity. A mix of voices, from advertising to activism, compete for attention'. It is said to be part of the fabric of the city, and an assortment of objects from billboard advertising, a construction hoarding, a highway sign, neighbourhood marker, signs, posters of various kinds (outdoor, subway, bus shelter), stickers, bus livery, and cab cards provide the concrete examples (1996: 15–28). This replicates the range of objects listed at the beginning of the chapter. It is important because it acknowledges what urban designers refer to using an array of terms. Lupton simply calls the same things graphic design.

From this a sense emerges of how the city 'speaks' in different voices, in different settings, in a media medley of messages designed to coax, influence and inform. These append human discourse and represent the variety of voices in the city, seen rather than heard as graphic language in the street. When graphic designers make these observations, the association between graphic design and urban public space stops at the point where a more in-depth understanding of the built environment could enhance the relationship further.

It should be clear by now that towards the end of the twentieth century, graphic design's adoption of and adaptation to diverse forms of expression, coupled with significant technological change, has hindered a concise portrayal of the field. When definitions did emerge in general dictionaries at the turn of the millennium, some activities such as film and public signage were still overlooked; the field lacked the cohesion to develop a linear approach to explaining how it was evolving. At this time, the purpose of graphic design became a focus of attention because of its persuasive and informative potential; beyond this there remained differences about what else it did: some prioritized instruction whilst others prioritized recreation.

Having been first introduced as a 'tool' for reinforcing concrete, these various portrayals of graphic design suggest that its foundations are yet to solidify. Yet historians claim it to be as old as cities and civilization.

In the name of graphic design

Amidst the evolving practice of graphic design in the late twentieth century, 1983 is a landmark year. In that year, graphic design was historicized as an academic pursuit and its origins, relationships with industry and cultural associations became evident. In *A History of Graphic Design* (Meggs 1983) explored its evolution from prehistoric times and the invention of writing; the development of printing in fifteenth-century Europe; the industrial revolution and new forms such as photography; to 'modern' graphic design in the twentieth century. Graphic design was then introduced – albeit in a very limited fashion – on the dust jacket as a 'concept' representing 'the art of books, advertising, packaging, propaganda, [and] corporate identity'. Not only did the various practices integrated within the field now have a sense of collective identity, a claim to longevity also confirmed its ancestry within the cradle of civilization.

Historical accounts of graphic design – of which there have since been others adding to the further editions of Meggs' tome (e.g. Drucker and McVarish 2013; Eskilson 2012; Hollis 2001; Jubert [2005] 2006) – trace the activity back at least 5,000 years to the invention of writing, and before then, to early markings made by pre-historic man in the form of cave paintings that incorporated dots, squares and other configurations. This is further substantiated by recent evidence of human mark-making in the form of drawing, painting and stencilling found on cave walls and ceilings dating back 40,000 years in Sulawesi, Indonesia (Ghosh 2014). Some 10,000–20,000 years later, simple abstract marks such as lines, dots, and concentric circles carved into Palaeolithic bones appear as far apart as France and Australia (Jubert [2005] 2006: 18) (representing events such as the lunar cycle).

From this starting point, graphic design historians trace the development of the field from antiquity up to the present day through the development of alphabets, illuminated manuscripts, invention of printing, the industrial revolution, the Arts and Crafts movement, the influence of modern art and the International Style, the information age, digital revolution, to 'do it yourself' and 'citizenship.' The origin of what we now call 'graphic design' at least 5,000 years ago in Sumeria follows a lineage with the establishment of urban design and architecture in Mesopotamia 10,000 years ago, and further back to the development of specialized tools 40,000 years ago (Friedman 1998: 85).

Aside from the integrative activity in the twentieth century, and claims to a past evidenced in the first known mark-making by humans on cave walls, graphic design connects to an increasingly complex and diverse range of activities. In the early twenty-first century, graphic designers nominate numerous professional activities in the name of graphic design. Table 2.4 lists the ways graphic designers select and combine visual 'elements', work towards visual 'goals', and negotiate 'effects' (adapted from van der Waarde 2009). Within this typography and illustration sit alongside newer activities such as desktop publishing, spatial design, and end-user research. As a professional activity it is said to be 'a commercial activity that develops visual means to support dialogue between clients and their contacts' (van der Waarde 2009: 5). Such descriptions privilege commerce over culture (overlooking Dwiggins' artistic aspirations) by positioning graphic design as a service for sale, alluding to the commercial art of the past from which early pioneers of graphic design tried to distance themselves. Whilst the professional performance of graphic design undoubtedly requires an understanding of commerce, the implication is that graphic design is done for profit or industry. This is a partial truth aligned with advertising as a visual goal, but it has diminished importance compared to the many other stated activities, upholding Dwiggins' suggestion that advertising design is just one of many forms of graphic design.

Clearly, the idea of graphic design is continually evolving and the range of activities and intentions undertaken in its name diminish and increase. No longer is calligraphy significant in the way Dwiggins considered it to be, but typography remains central. No longer is printing the dominant media, but screen communication is in the ascendant. No longer is graphic design undertaken only by individuals, but also by large teams who fulfil multiple junior and senior roles across a spectrum of expertise. No longer is

TABLE 2.4   The activity of graphic designers

Visual elements	Visual goals	Effects
Illustration	Film production	Marketing
Photography	Website design	Communication strategy
Typography	Graphic art	Usability
Copywriting	Spatial design	End-user research
Image processing	Advertising	Visual research
Animation	House style design	Visual strategy
Audio-video		Concept development
Programming		House style management
Author		Project organization
Infographics		
Font design		
Desktop publishing		

it about the present and future, but also the past, with an established and continually evolving history. Interpretations differ from country to country. For example, in Portugal, semantics still link the graphic designer (designer gráfico) closely with the printing industry (indústria gráfica).

Increased consciousness aroused by a continually expanding perception has led to proclamations that it is widespread, 'everywhere, touching everything we do, we see, everything we buy' (Helfland 2001: 137). Such claims further hinder definition and place it in conflict with other design activities such as architecture. Nonetheless, the extent of what can be called graphic design in modern life is clear. It is pervasive, and plays a significant part in what Moles (1989: 119) refers to as the small-scale anxieties, pleasures, structures, events and decisions within everyday life.

Moles uses the idea of graphic design in its most comprehensive sense: to define the 'legibility of the world', representing things, products and actions through the ability to translate life into 'intelligible discourse'. This positions graphic design as 'signs', or 'symbolic element shapes' such as 'arrows, shingles, posters, signals, . . . the door, . . . the corporate identity, the logotype, the traffic sign'. Graphic design is said to connect with the environment both through its social function and communication capacity, exposing the two spatial distinctions Moles (1989) identifies as *real space* and *the printed page*. By real space, he suggests spaces and volumes such as 'boulevards, hallways, streets, train stations, piers, sidewalks, stairs, shop windows, signs, household shells, offices, work places'. These are all perceptible because they are 'symbolically marked' and become symbols, whereas the printed page refers to the standardized sizes for paper or posters that the graphic designer fills through 'graphic engineering' and the use of 'line, contrast, shape, right angle, texture, color [sic] as graphic units' or '*symbol atoms*'. From this perspective of psychology and sociology, Moles offers a further description by stating 'Graphic design is, generally speaking, the science and the technique of establishing a functional equivalency between a message and its purpose . . . to maximise the impact of communication through the combined or disjointed means of the written message, the sign, or the image' (Moles 1989: 120). Once again, we see the distancing of art in favour, this time, of science, but it is not something that can be measured. It's worth noting here that Moles' attempt to discern the spaces graphic design occupies – real and printed – is similar to the relationship analogized by Kevin Lynch who attempted to explain legibility by contrasting the simplicity of page design with the difficulty of city design (1989: 122). We return to this in Chapter 4.

Attempting to answer the question 'What is graphic design?' by reviewing a selection of claims that describe it, leads to the conclusion that it has, so far, been a fluid practice. Collectively, it is described as the art, science, technique, and skill, allied to the origination, arrangement and combination of specialist activities with impact and communicative intention. It is not media or discipline-specific, and does not have spatial or temporal boundaries. Asking the question in 1954 provides a different answer in 2014. The shortest definitions insufficiently limit its intention, scope and application, whereas wider interpretations – from outside art and design – speak of it having symbolising and spatial qualities. Symbolism in the form of images or objects is generally understood, but the spatial dimension beyond the arrangement of graphic entities on a page, to use one of Moles' distinctions, is less known. This connection between graphic design and *real* space is where the associations with urban context become concrete and as much a spatial practice.

Graphic design as a spatial practice

All previously discussed, accounts recognize and establish graphic design as a universal portmanteau practice, but the sheer variety of applications – from picturing in caves using digits to picturing on screens using digital technology – make it fundamentally a spatial-temporal phenomenon. Its temporal dimension is revealed as history through accounts of graphic design before and after the name surfaced in the early twentieth century (this is explored further in Chapter 2). Through time, the inventive use of graphic communication has been documented from stencil to screen, but this is more than a physical tracing exercise; it is the outcome of human endeavour and a representation of who we are as people. As Soja (2010: 15) puts it: 'It is over time that we also create our collective selves, construct the societies and cultures, polities and economies within which our individual experiences are expressed and inscribed.' Such expressions and inscriptions are manifested through graphic design. Soja suggests that scholars and the wider public view history as 'more revealing and insightful than thinking spatially or geographically' (2010: 15).

With this in mind, and to further understand graphic design as a spatial practice with social connotations, explanations will next be borrowed from geography and philosophy, and applied to graphic design within an urban context in order to grasp the notion of graphic design as a spatial practice. This will differ from the notion of graphic space as either the graphic representation of space through marks on a surface or as a depiction of spatial structure. The former means the organization of different marks whereas the latter denotes a two-dimensional or three-dimensional illusion of space in the way a bridge is shown to cross a river on a map (von Engelhardt 2002: 21), or the way a letterform is drawn to suggest three dimensionality. Nevertheless, this latter interpretation of graphic space applies to graphic design as a spatial practice in the way it depends on mental constructions and visual perception.

According to Thrift, space is the 'stuff' of geography, and is conceived in four ways: (1) as an 'empirical construction'; (2) as a 'flow space'; (3) as an 'image space'; and (4) as 'place space' (2009: 85–96). This is referred to as a *relational* view of space' – an idea 'undergoing continual construction as a result of the agency of things encountering each other in more-or-less organized circulations.' In simpler terms, this means the way actions are supported in an integrated system, and graphic design is present in this action.

With regard to the first space, as *empirical constructions* ordinary objects such as a typeface, clock face, or computer interface construct spaces. Thrift also lists 'houses, cars, mobiles, knives and forks, offices, bicycles, computers, clothes and dryers, cinemas, trains, televisions, garden paths'. These material objects are what Moles called the 'universal elements of daily life,' symbolized by the imposition of symbolic elements to provide a 'knowledge through signs' (1989: 120). We can take this to mean either the application of graphic elements such as name or symbol, perhaps combined in a brandmark, or the properties the object itself possesses, such as a distinctive colour, shape, texture or pattern. For example, the design of the original Apple iMac G3 with its soft egg-shape form and translucent plastic case is a symbolic interpretation.

As a *flow space*, graphic design gives physical and virtual form to the movement of information, connecting people to people and people to place. Closely aligned with the interconnected notion of globalization, information as mediated communication brings together entities otherwise disconnected, such as the facility to access a website.

Image space is the third and most obviously related conception of space to graphic design because of the image saturated capacity. Thrift lists a variety of images 'from paintings to photographs, from portraits to postcards, from religious icons to pastoral landscapes, from collages to pastiches, from the simplest of graphs to the most complex animations', testifying that the pervasive 'picture' provides us with a space register. In particular, he highlights the screens (television and computer) that inhabit our homes, bars, airports, stations, cafés, shops, shopping centres, waiting rooms, dealing rooms, offices, studies and bedrooms as constructions of space. All of these spaces contain graphic images of one kind or another.

Finally, *place space* asks us to 'think of a walk in the city which consists not just of eye making contact with other people or advertising signs or buildings, but also the sound of traffic noise and conversation, the touch of ticket machine and hand rail, the smell of exhaust fumes and cooking food'. These are all symbols, signs, and representations, and Thrift uses the conjoined phrase 'a-where-ness', accentuating *affect* as crucial in understanding place as space. Graphic design distinctly contributes to this notion of a-where-ness in all four of the geographer's conceptualization of space.

This relational view of space, or *relational* space, fuses actions with systems, and is inherently graphic. It also endorses an understanding of space as explained by Lefebvre as 'directly lived through its associated images and symbols' that 'tend towards more or less coherent systems of non-verbal symbols and signs . . . Art works, writing systems, fabrics, and so on' (1991: 39–43). The products of graphic design contribute to what Lefebvre calls 'the production of space' as a social reality, or 'a set of relations and forms' (1991: 116), constituted as 'maps and plans, transport and communication systems, information conveyed by images and signs' called 'representations of space' (1991: 233). These two interpretations of space, as social reality or set of relationships, divide graphic objects as entities in their own right or graphic objects as part of the urban fabric. Lefebvre further explained this as part of a 'conceptual triad', comprising:

1   *Spatial practice*, which embraces production and reproduction, and the particular locations and spatial sets characteristic of each social formation. Spatial practice ensures continuity and some degree of cohesion. In terms of social space, and of each member of a given society's relationship to that space, this cohesion implies a guaranteed level of *competence* and a specific level of *performance*.

2   *Representations of space*, which are tied to the relations of production and to the 'order' which those relations impose, and hence to knowledge, to signs, to codes, and to 'frontal' relations.

3   *Representational space*, which embody complex symbolisms, sometimes coded, sometimes not, linked to the clandestine or underground side of social life, as also to art (which may come eventually to be defined less as a code of space than a code of representational spaces).

LEFEBVRE 1991: 33

Within this triad, continuity, cohesion, competence, performance, order, symbolisms and art are terms that also identify graphic design as a spatial practice. Lefebvre foregrounds systems, images and symbols, relationships and forms, and representations as social reality, but further introduces a new interpretation of what representation might be. The 'space of images, and photographs, as of drawings and plans' is what he calls 'visual space' (1991: 298). Representations of space and visual space appear to be the same except the former is directed towards an urban action. Thus, representational space, representations of space, visual space, and spatial practice provide frameworks for considering the products of graphic design as systems, images, symbols, relations and forms.

This portrayal of graphic design as a spatial practice is legitimized in portrayals of space in disciplines other than graphic design or art and design. Geography provides a further perspective directly linked to facets of graphic design.

Beyond graphic design

Although graphic design is predominantly associated with art and design, at least in higher education, there has been significant expansion, added depth and diversification of the field since the early 1990s, accommodating many new points of view. As well as the advances in art and design history charting new influences, such as post-modernism (e.g. Poyner 2003), others have approached the field with a concern for communication (e.g. Barnard 2005). Hence, graphic design has become as much appreciated for its idiosyncratic unruly aesthetic or the contrasting orderly influence of modernism, as its relationship to communication, meaning, function, audiences and markets, global reach and art. Thus, variation of provision in art and design higher education is now manifest in all manner of programme titles that emphasize specialization such as illustration, typography or animation, technological bias through digital media, motion graphics or multi-media. There has been an aspiration to link with other academic fields such as visual communication and communication design (Harland 2012), as well as new disciplines such as visual culture. Yet, cross-disciplinary interests where there are obvious graphic synergies, for example the geographer's use of 'graphicacy', have been overlooked (Harland 2015b: 87–97). It is relatively unknown that disciplines as far apart as mathematics and literary criticism both acknowledge the notion of 'graphicality'. Computational mathematics (Del Genio *et al.* 2011), cognitive science (Shimojima 1999), and textual studies (Eaves 2002) all make use of the word, first used by Edgar Allan Poe when describing a passage in Margaret Fuller's writing in *Summer on the Lakes* about Niagara (1843: 5). Poe proclaims:

> Many of the descriptions in this volume are unrivalled for graphicality, (why is there not such a word?) for the force with which they convey the true by the novel or unexpected, by the introduction of touches which other artists would be sure to omit as irrelevant to the subject. This faculty, too, springs from her subjectiveness, which leads her to paint a scene less by its features than by its effects.
>
> POE 1858: 74

For our purpose here, the most useful of these various interpretations is geography's use of graphicacy, in part because it is defined as a communication competency. The term comes from the work of geographers Balchin and Coleman, who in 1965 published the article *Graphicacy should be the Fourth Ace in the Pack* in *The Times Educational Supplement* (5 November) (this is a year earlier than cited by some geographers, who will have seen an article of the same name in *The Cartographer*, 3: 23–8, 1966). In 1972 Balchin gave a precise definition as 'the communication of spatial information that cannot be conveyed adequately by verbal [meaning written rather than spoken] or numerical means' (Boardman 1983: preface). Initially, they called for more teaching of the subject in primary school, but it has since been adopted as a research method in the university teaching of geography.

Whereas cartography has as its focus all issues relating to mapping and maps – 'development, production, dissemination and study of maps' – graphicacy is concerned with the 'skills of reading and constructing graphic modes of communication, such as maps, diagrams and pictures' (Perkins 2003: 343). It is claimed as one of four geographic competencies alongside articulacy, literacy and numeracy, as the 'fluency in the construction and interpretation of graphic modes of communication (graphs, diagrams, illustrations, photographs, sculpture, icons, and maps)' (Monmonier 1993: 4–12).

Although not as much understood as literacy or numeracy, it is notable for its inclusion of sculpture, but the omission of typography and lettering, possibly due to the fact that despite its importance on maps, lettering is considered a difficult area for cartographers (Perkins 2003: 358). Others suggest that 'graphicacy is a form of communication in that it utilises some form of symbolic language to convey information about spatial relationships. Graphic representations include maps, photographs, pictures, diagrams, cartoons, sketches, posters and graphs' (Wilmot 1999: 91). Its foundation is based in what Wilmot (1999) notes as 'spatial perception and spatial conceptualization' through which 'one makes sense of one's experiences'. Wilmot goes on to say:

> The process is twofold: firstly, it relates to the gathering of information through the senses about what objects are in the environment and where they are; secondly, it relates to a process of organisation that takes place in the brain so as to order and make sense of the messages conveyed through the senses about the world.
>
> 1999: 93

The reading and construction dimension of graphicacy, allied to information gathering, object definition, orientation, and cognitive sense making suggests a close affiliation with the products and process of graphic design. Within the context of the arguments set out in this chapter, there is a strong justification for the notion of *urban graphicacy* as a communication competency. The products of this can be called *urban graphic objects*; these are further explained at the beginning of Chapter 3. In the meantime, throughout this book, an urban graphic object means a graphic object directly associated with the functioning of the urban environment. For example, a pedestrian sign that directs you to a city destination is an urban graphic object, but a magazine is not. While it may be interpreted as a graphic object, a magazine may only indirectly influence human behaviour in cities.

There is some evidence of graphic objects in the world of digital software as something created using 'pens', 'brushes' and 'fonts'. Graphic objects, in the form of lines, arcs, circles and rectangles are also associated with mathematical formulae. In art, graphic objects are associated with Mira Schendel's work on the way paper, lettering, poetry, acrylic laminate mounts, transparency and philosophy combine in aesthetic abstract form, rather than readable, meaning-making compositions.

Where readable meaning-making compositions are concerned, the most comprehensive explanation of what a graphic object is can be found in the work of von Engelhardt (2002), as part of a wider discussion about graphic syntax and *The Language of Graphics*. Graphic objects are synonymous with graphic representations, integrating 'the recursive notion of *composite graphic objects* and their *graphic sub-objects*' (2002: 23, original italics). Essentially, this translates as the recurring relationship between the whole object and the parts of the object on different layers, which at the most detailed level, are referred to as 'elementary graphic objects'. This recursive nature is inherent in the following definition:

> A *composite graphic object* consists of a graphic space that contains a set of *graphic-sub-objects*. A graphic sub-object may be a composite graphic object itself, or it may be an elementary graphic object.
>
> VON ENGELHARDT 2002: 23, original italics

Von Engelhardt exemplifies the concept of the graphic object using a sign, for instance comprising a white pictogram of a bicycle contained within a blue circular background (see Plate 1). The pictogram and circle are each elementary graphic objects. More complex examples, such as a map, are said to have multiple sub-objects on several levels. Graphic representations as graphic objects are explained as a 'nesting' phenomenon to accommodate the recursive nature of the idea, emphasizing object-to-space relationships and object-to-object relationships in a recursive 'syntactic decomposition' (2002: 14–15). In sum, a graphic object is ventured as:

- an elementary graphic object, or
- a composite graphic object, consisting of:
    - a graphic space that is occupied by it, and
    - a set of graphic objects, which are contained within that graphic space, and
    - a set of graphic relations in which these graphic objects are involved.

At each level, a graphic object is characterized by 'visual attributes' such as size, shape or colour. Drawing from the work of Kepes (1944) and Bertin ([1967] 1983), von Engelhardt proposes that 'a visual attribute is a visually perceivable attribute of a graphic object' (2002: 25) and, for convenience, divides these into spatial attributes (orientation, shade, size, plane) and area-fill attributes (value, grain, colour), providing detailed explanations of what these stand for.

These structural aspects are explained as part of a comprehensive framework that also includes semiotic aspects and the classification of graphic representations, with a focus on static graphic language, or '*schemas*'. Von Engelhardt's emphasis is on graphic representations such as 'ancient maps and Egyptian hieroglyphs, but also family tree diagrams, pictorial statistical charts, and modern 3-D computer visualizations, and leads us to a working definition: 'a graphic representation is a visible artefact on a more or less flat surface, that was created in order to express information' (2002: 2). This serves a purpose, but is too narrow for our aspirations in that we also emphasize three dimensions. For example, von Engelhardt dismisses a real-world model of a molecule as a graphic representation, but would include a drawing. We include both. There is also a restriction on 'information' whereas we treat this as one of the six functions of graphic representation (outlined in Chapter 6). Furthermore, the visual attributes listed above overlook the most fundamental aspect of graphic representation: line. We look towards a more expressive, or artistic, analysis of visual language that identifies the principle visual elements of line, shape, tone, colour, texture, form, scale, space and light within an environment (Cohen and Anderson 2006: 9–12). For convenience, and to varying degrees, we treat the first six of these as intrinsic attributes or properties of a graphic object whereas scale, space and light will be considered as external factors in that they are more context-dependent relational qualities.

Summary

This chapter has exposed the difficulty urban thinkers have in categorizing forms of communication other than as transport infrastructure. It has focused on another interpretation of communication and another set of objects that have been difficult to name and qualify. With a focus on how to study cities, a partial perspective has been introduced to frame a way of thinking about the city through adopting a graphic design stance.

Art and design perspectives on the physical character of the city have been shown to be difficult to define due to the variety of subjects represented, which may be as diverse as fashion, film or fine arts. Consequently, a discussion about how perspectives may be formed from design theory and its concern for systemics led to the selective starting point of graphic design for studying the city as a partial system. Thus, graphic design, a subject closely associated with art and design, has been adopted as a stance for framing a study into the array of urban objects that have hitherto been neglected.

Although exposed as an immature academic discipline and not easily defined, graphic design has been introduced as an activity directly associated with urban public space, and a significant contributor to making the world legible through its symbolizing spatial capability. This is also where graphic design and graphic design theory relate to the disciplinary concerns of geography, its preoccupation with space, and how this is realized through graphicacy. There is clearly an opportunity to explore how design and social science may combine to develop a sense of urban graphicacy, concerning fluency in the way urban graphic communication is conceived, planned and made for the urban context. The phrase *urban graphic object* – adding graphic as a premodifier to the urban design use of urban object – has been used as one way of framing studies into a universal phenomena that has until now been neglected.

Wide in scope, graphic design has been acknowledged as being connected to urban public space through formal and informal messages. But interpretations of graphic design are not fixed – they invariably suggest a collaborative activity concerned with a visual form of communication that aspires to be holistic. It incorporates specialist activities such as typography, illustration and photography, but is distinct from these. It is both generative and organizing. A multitude of definitions and descriptions that change depending on emergent applications and different perspectives have been discussed, but as time progresses, we appear to move further away from Dwiggins' use of graphic design and his aspiration for artistry lessens. We will return to this in Chapter 3.

When graphic design is explained as a spatial practice, and aligned with graphicacy and its concern for conveying spatial information, this new perspective provides a framework for exploring the relationship between graphic design and urban public space, as urban graphicacy. This provides a distinct partial design perspective on urban systems. Having established a stance for framing urban graphic objects, born out of a viewpoint made up of transdisciplinary perspectives, Chapter 3 examines the urban graphic object in history, and in so doing, will define the urban, while focusing on examples that exemplify longevity, scope, scale, and space.

3

History

*'An object is anything that can be indicated, anything that is
pointed to or referred to . . . '.*

BLUMER 1969: 10

Introduction

Chapter 2 identified a bewildering array of miscellaneous urban objects and how these
may be better collectively characterized through graphic design. This chapter develops
this theme, but looks more closely at the urban context and how history has reported on
the phenomena. It will feature two examples, 2,000 years apart, but linked through
aesthetic considerations that expound on the unifying aspirations of Roman inscription
and twentieth-century typeface design that demonstrates a sense of permanence.
Furthermore, the chapter reviews how interest in the topic has evolved since the Second
World War, revealing how inadequate this has been compared to the pace of change in
cities. The aim is to clarify the historical scope of interest in order to then establish how
urban graphic objects contribute to the image of the city. But first, we extend the urban
designers notion of the urban object to explain what an urban graphic object is.

The urban graphic object

Positioning the word 'graphic' in the middle of the existing phrase 'urban object', as
used in urban design, provides both a filter for enhancing the visual dimension of urban
design and a lens through which a more meaningful contribution can be made to
understanding urban systems from art and design. Putting the word urban aside for
the moment to further concentrate on graphic objects, in addition to what has been
proposed at the end of Chapter 2, graphic implies something vivid in the way ideas,
concepts, feelings and thoughts are pictured and portrayed, written and wrought. As
was argued in Chapter 1, it can define a spatial communication competency. The word

'object' implies something concrete, but may also be the something to which an action or feeling is directed (as will be discussed in Chapter 6) or a sense of purpose. Throughout this book 'object' means material thing.

To fully benefit from using the phrase graphic object with the prefix urban requires both abstract and literal interpretations of what a graphic object can be. For example, in semiotics, the Roman alphabet is judged to be part of an evolved abstract writing system dependent entirely on learned meaning. The word *man* is a 'symbolic' (abstract) representation, whereas a photograph of a man is an 'iconic' (literal) representation. This is explained further in Chapter 6 when we look at semiotics.

The phrase 'urban graphic object' is favoured here because none of the words and phrases used by urban thinkers as listed at the beginning of the previous chapter extend far enough to categorize the phenomena in that they each represent another partial perspective, often conjuring up ambiguity or simply naming things. Nor have these emerged from an art and design perspective. Graphic design is yet to fully explore the extent of its contribution to the urban environment despite established histories of graphic design having been developed since the early 1980s. The history of graphic design will soon be examined for evidence of its urban impact, but first the nature of the urban will be clarified, as will urban design.

What is urban (design)?

Having outlined briefly what an *urban graphic object* is by explaining how graphic and object come together, this section concentrates on the earlier part of that phrase: urban. In doing so, we will link urban to design and start to define more exactly what urban design is, so that further links between graphic design and urban design can be more fully understood to provide an important sense of context.

Examining urban form from a graphic design perspective requires clarification about what urban means. There is no simple definition for the term urban. Essentially, it stands for the characteristics of towns and cities. Hence, *city* is interchangeably linked to the Latin *urbs/urbis*, and *oppidum* (town) or *oppidulum* (small town). The origin of city is in the Greek word *polis*, as used in the word *metropolis*, meaning mother (*mētēr*) city (*polis*). Both city and town are captured in the Latin *urbānus*, and the urban is directly associated with *oppidānus* (provincial). In simpler categorical terms, a city is a large town, this being a settlement larger than a village. Hence, 'downtown' refers to the oldest part of a city where there is likely to be a concentration of business and shopping facilities. In Britain, a city traditionally needed the additional qualifying presence of a cathedral, but this is no longer the case. Thus, to study the urban environment is to look at and consider cities and towns from an historical and contemporary perspective. This includes not only the difference between towns and cities, but also across a rural to urban continuum, which is similarly ill-defined as it overlooks a need to accommodate suburbs.

For approximately 10,000 years, humans have lived in rural and urban environments of varying size and complexity, on a scale from the smallest isolated place to what is now the megacity/metacity comprising formal and informal habitats spread across enormous city territories connected by information technology and communication systems. Even beyond that, we now have 'megaregions', such as SãoRio combining São Paulo and Rio de Janeiro, one of the drivers of world economy (Leite, 2013: 198). It is widely thought that human settlement first happened when groups of migratory people evolved into sedentary farmers by domesticating animals and cultivating cereal crops, changing their nomadic lifestyle into a more stable community-based specialized existence. But the isolated and dispersed nature of cities as they emerged in Mesopotamia, India, Egypt, China, Central America and Peru suggest factors other than food surplus played a role.

Settlement types (of which at least eight are known) sit on a continuum between rural and urban, but defining the line that separates one settlement type from another, physically or socially, is no longer thought to be possible and an urban–rural continuum represents a graduation between one extreme of total rurality and another of total urbanity, as depicted in Figure 3.1 (Waugh 2000: 388). It seems most commonly understood that the rural–urban transition happens at the scale of the town (small to large), and the town's importance is reinforced by the prominence given to it by some prominent urban thinkers (e.g. Burke 1976; Cullen 1971; Rykwert 1988).

In numerical terms, the UK Government suggest that rural places in England and Wales be defined settlements of less than 10,000 to 1,500 people, this being the smallest comprising an urban place (Anon 2004). The Government's Statistical Services has since revised the rural–urban classification in England to six rural and four urban settlement/context types. See Figure 3.2. This conforms to urban being defined as more than 10,000 people and rural areas being less, or being open countryside, introducing a typology comprising: hamlets and isolated dwellings; villages; town and fringe; city and town; minor conurbation; and major conurbation, some sparsely populated and others not. Produced for the 2011 Census, the scheme acknowledges that a simple statistical split alone is insufficient, and density profiles are factored in to account for sparsely populated rural and urban areas. Produced primarily for statistical analysis, this may cover 'a large area of open countryside and yet be still urban if most of the population live in an urban settlement. Rural is a matter of settlement form and dwelling density rather than the economic function or the character or use of the land' (Anon 2013).

Furthermore, definitions of 'urban' vary from country to country. An official definition of urban for the United Kingdom is: 'Built-up areas (of at least 20 hectares of built-up land) with 10,000 or more people living in them' whereas the United States of America stipulates 'Agglomerations of 2,500 or more inhabitants, generally having population densities of 1,000 persons per square mile or more'. Some places require as few as 200 inhabitants (Greenland, Iceland, Norway) and the Falkland Islands (Malvinas) simply defines urban as the Town of Stanley! Direct comparison of urban areas is

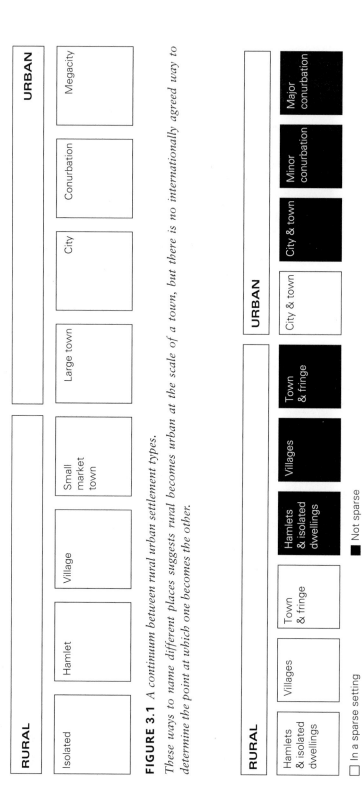

RURAL					URBAN		
Isolated	Hamlet	Village	Small market town	Large town	City	Conurbation	Megacity

FIGURE 3.1 *A continuum between rural urban settlement types.*

These ways to name different places suggests rural becomes urban at the scale of a town, but there is no internationally agreed way to determine the point at which one becomes the other.

RURAL				URBAN		
Hamlets & isolated dwellings	Villages	Town & fringe		City & town		
Hamlets & isolated dwellings	Villages	Town & fringe		City & town	Minor conurbation	Major conurbation

☐ In a sparse setting   ■ Not sparse

FIGURE 3.2 *Rural-urban classification of census output areas in the UK.*

Recent attempts to define the rural-urban relationship are more nuanced and take into account the density of population.

therefore difficult, as these may be determined by administration, politics, population size or density, economy or the quality of streets, lighting or sewerage (Aslam and Szczuka 2012: 10).

Considered on a global scale, an urban environment could be any environment from a hamlet to a megacity and urban graphic objects extend across the whole scale of settlement types, be it the number of a house, the name of a cottage in a remote field, or the significantly more sophisticated system of postal/zip codes across a large megacity. This starts to suggest that if graphic objects are acts of urban design, the scale of thinking across all settlement types is significant.

Having argued for a graphic design perspective on urban systems, an obvious point where graphic design meets the urban is through design, or more specifically urban design. One of the objectives of this book is to establish the idea of graphic design as urban design. But what is urban design when definitions of urban are so imprecise? This is a more complex question but it can be answered by looking at some basic definitions, and venturing how these relate to our purpose here.

Lang (1994: ix) affirms that urban design is 'a relatively new term for an activity of long standing . . . concerned with the design of the four dimensional physical layout of human settlements and their parts'. Moreover, it is an 'art', and Lang cites Clarence Stein's 1955 description of urban design as 'the art of relating: STRUCTURES to one another and to their NATURAL SETTING to serve CONTEMPORARY LIVING' adding 'in' and 'over time'. He goes on to say it is 'the art of relating one set of professional concerns to other sets' (a fitting intention for this book). A simpler interpretation is 'Everything you can see out of the window' (Carmona *et al.* 2010: 4, citing Tibbalds 1988a) offering an open invitation to call everything urban design, including graphic objects. More detailed though is:

> . . . urban design should be taken to mean the relationship between different buildings; the relationship between buildings and the streets, squares, parks and waterways and other spaces which make up the public domain; the nature and quality of the public domain itself; the relationship of one part of a village, town or city with other parts; and the patterns of movement and activity which are thereby established: in short, the complex relationships between all the elements of built and unbuilt space.
>
> CABE 2001: 18, citing Planning Policy Guidance Note 1

This final sentence is clearly inclusive, but of most significance to our interests here, is the importance placed on how the different parts of urban environments are related, and the patterns of movement and activity. Graphic objects facilitate this. Furthermore, urban design is 'the *process* of making *better* places for people *than would otherwise be produced*' (Carmona *et al.* 2010: 3, original italics), putting emphasis on aspiration. The scope is clearly wide, but at its core is a concern for relationships and the integration of different kinds of knowledge, understanding and skills. Structure and objects suggest material things, and all elements are included in this, whereas movement and activity signals human behaviour. Clearly, there is enough flexibility in these descriptions to build firm links with graphic design and contemplate *graphic design as urban design*. But where in the scope of urban design might this relationship be best understood? This can happen in different ways and with a number of beneficiaries.

Graphic design adds value to urban environments through economic, social and environmental benefits. For example, it can contribute to economic prosperity by making development more competitive at relatively low cost, contribute to urban regeneration and place marketing, and differentiate places by increasing their prestige (see case studies on Ghirardelli Square in San Francisco, and the Theater District and Times Square in New York). Furthermore, social and environmental benefits will come from the role of graphic design in creating well connected, inclusive and accessible places, sensitivity towards local context, adherence to safety and security, enhancing civic image, and by revitalising urban heritage (see case studies on Johnston's 'Underground' Typeface, Shinjuku Ward in Tokyo, City of Westminster street nameplate, London, and Ornamentation [as Unification] in Lisbon). There are several beneficiaries including investors, developers, designers, occupiers, everyday users and society as a whole, and public authorities (CABE 2001: 9).

Specific examples include the significant contribution that street signs make to the local charm and character of an area, as well as historic street furniture including monuments, plaques and memorials, traffic signs and signals that do not add clutter, appropriately designed bollards; signs as part of the architecture, historically sensitive telephone kiosks and postboxes, and new design that is fit for purpose, durable, low maintenance and fitting the context (Davies and Wagner 2000). The most important of these for identifying the locality of where we live, street signs, benefits from local variation in design, material and lettering for adding richness and variety to the street scene. In some instances retaining and restoring old signs enhance historic continuity. See Figure 3.3 for a selection of signs sensitive to local context. This is a design detail but appropriate signage is something that makes significant difference in street design (CABE 2002: 30–31).

Because urban design is such a broad field concerned with enhancing place making for people, its various integrated contexts, dimensions, implementation and delivery mechanisms suggest that some aspects more than others are suited to a focused discussion about graphic design as urban design. The design context for urban design involves a number of all-embracing conditions that include local, global, market and regulatory factors; these, in turn, influence urban design principles and practice. These are explained in detail by Carmona *et al.* (2003), framed as defining dimensions of urban design in the guise of 'morphological', 'perceptual', 'social', 'visual', 'functional' and 'temporal'.

Local, global, market and regulatory matters play a role in determining the nature of urban graphic objects, be it in the form of a Coca-Cola logotype on the side of a vending machine (global), hand lettering on a city wall in ancient Rome (local), an illuminated

FIGURE 3.3 *Street signs that add local charm and character (Valencia, Spain 2014; Paris, France 2015; San Francisco, USA 2013; Rome, Italy 2009; Umeå, Sweden 2014; London, UK 2015; Bath, UK 2010; San Francisco, USA, 2013; Longano, Italy 2009; Leeds, UK 2014).*

The name of a street may be displayed in a variety of designs that utilize different lettering styles, materials and applications, to sign streets across the full scale of settlement types.

peep show signboard (market), or a parking restriction sign (regulatory). The defining dimensions of urban design similarly encapsulate graphic objects. These dimensions are briefly paraphrased below because their definitions invite suggestions about how graphic design is embedded within urban design. In addition, a clarifying statement with exemplars in *italic* are added in brackets:

Morphological dimension: concerned with change in the physical form and shape of settlements over time, it is also about the configuration of urban form and shape, and the spatial patterns of infrastructure that support it. [Infrastructure in this sense is more related to land use, building structure, plot patterns, street patterns, grids, how buildings and space mutually define each other, road hierarchy and use of space. *Urban graphic objects define road hierarchy reflected in the colour coding of street signs.*]

Perceptual dimension: concerned with environmental images, symbolism, and meaning in the built environment, and 'sense of place', place image and place identity. [Most of this dimension is pertinent; in particular Lynch's image of the city is a contested idea. *Urban graphic objects feature in four of Lynch's five city elements illustrated by the authors: a pedestrian crossing, deckchair, street nameplate and retail fascia. The exception is landmarks.*]

Social dimension: concerned with society and space, this is framed as the relationship between people and environment, and how human behaviour and the physical environment affect each other. [An emphasis on public life and the public realm aligned to human need situate this dimension as dependent on graphic elements. *Urban graphic objects comprise of regulatory signs or uniformed police officers.*]

Visual dimension: concerned with the urban environment's visual–aesthetic character, and the shift from civic to urban design, its focus is on the integrated spatial (volumetric) and visual qualities, the artefacts within and their relationship to each other. Aesthetic preference, visual–aesthetic qualities and the design of elements that define and occupy urban space are three main discussion points. [This dimension is the most appropriate for the purpose of this book in that it is directly concerned with facade, floorscape, street furniture, and public art. *Urban graphic objects dominate the look of many streets in cities such as Tokyo.*]

Functional dimension: concerned with how places work and how they can develop in terms of movement, 'people places', environmental design, healthier environments, and infrastructure. [People movement is a core activity facilitated by graphic design. *Urban graphic objects are essential to the public engagement with transport infrastructure.*]

Temporal dimension: concerned with the fourth dimension of time, change of use, continuity and stability, and new projects and policies are all considerations here. [This dimension is fundamentally present in any discussion about urban graphic objects. *Urban graphic objects date places and spaces in time.*]

CARMONA *et al.* 2010: 77–266

Urban graphic objects infiltrate all six dimensions of urban design and the remainder of this book will emphasize the visual dimension of urban design. Chapters 4 and 5 will expand on this by exploring familiar urban design concepts by Kevin Lynch (Imageability) and Christopher Alexander (Pattern), first introduced in the 1960s.

We have already established that definitions of the word city accommodate the importance of town, as does the origin of the word urban. In this book we are primarily concerned with the urban rather than the rural, but examples will be drawn from across the spectrum of settlement types on the basis that both spatial and temporal factors contribute to the development of urban environments, most cities once being smaller settlements. Throughout history, humans have interacted with their habitat and as settlements continue to expand, so too do the number of parts and perspectives that help us understand the city. However, history provides a meagre account of the role and importance of graphic communication in urban environments. Thus, the next section reviews the association between graphic design and urban history.

Graphic design's urban history

Despite the emergence of graphic design history towards the latter part of the twentieth century, it has not yet concerned itself with urban development. Its main focus has been on the products of graphic representation too numerous to mention, but which range from the early development of writing systems, to printed objects and, more recently, designs in digital media. For example, the early development of writing systems as a product of the city's administrative function feature in the early part of historians' accounts of graphic design. In this section we look at how graphic design historians, specifically Jubert ([2005] 2006) and Meggs and Purvis (2006) implicitly identify graphic design with the urban context at the 'dawn of civilisation' and, more recently, in the late nineteenth and twentieth centuries, but without much in between.

Chapter 2 explained graphic design as a form of representation and an approach for understanding and looking at the world. This stance identified historically with the earliest known human mark-making, supposedly made over 200,000 years ago in Africa (Meggs and Purvis 2006: 4) preceding evidence of the earliest physical setting for picture making in caves – the most explicit early form of graphic communication some 40,000 years ago. Abstract incisions on animal bones found in France have been dated to 20,000–30,000 years ago and literal representations of animals engraved on a deer antler have been traced to 15,000 years ago. Before the evolution of writing systems approximately 5,000 years ago as pictographic inscription in clay, a diversity of marks, proto-inscriptions, and ante-historical signs made by humans represented their practices in 'art, shamanism, commemoration, communication, divination, magic, mnemonics, mythology, mythography, and ornamentation, as well as relationships to the afterlife and to ritual and symbolism' (Jubert [2005] 2006: 18).

As well as humans developing their capacity to make marks, they simultaneously learned how to interpret them. For example, the imprint of an animal's paw on the floor as an aid to hunting provided a '*graphic sign*' (Hollis 2001: 7). Prehistoric humans concurrently developed skills not in reading and writing, or what we now call 'literacy' (writing as we know it today not having been invented) but more closely associated with reading and 'wrighting' – the ability to interpret and *make* meaningful marks. Jubert ([2005] 2006: 19) refers to this as 'art and visual expression' in the form of 'parietal paintings or drawings, of notches and incisions, or of *sculpture*', resembling what was earlier discussed in Chapter 2 as 'graphicacy'. Today, graphic design happens in the long shadow of these earlier human achievements.

The earliest association graphic design historians make between what we accentuate here as graphic design and urban design is the development of writing systems at the same time that cities emerged in Mesopotamia and Egypt around 3200 BCE respectively in the form of pictographs and hieroglyphics. As the city emerged as a unit of settlement with surplus production and a need for administration, it is speculated that writing played a significant role in the move from 'barbarism' to 'civilization'. In these cities, writing evolved as part of an accounting process, for example recording the number of sheep and cows in pictographic form, arranged in an orderly fashion using grids in horizontal and vertical rows. We will not recount here the development of writing systems that emerged from cities in Egypt, Mesopotamia, and the Indus valley areas – this is well documented by others – but what is important is the way writing became embedded into the urban fabric sometime in the nineteenth century BCE, in the form of imprinted foundation bricks used in Lower Mesopotamia (Jubert [2005] 2006: 21). From this point onwards, the city became the central place for the evolution of a glyphic-graphic urban phenomena. Objects with varying degrees of permanence integrate with the urban fabric, and although not all citizens are able to interpret the emerging sophisticated integrated forms of visual language, public places start to function as information display spaces. For example, in the public spaces of cities in Mesopotamia, official information such as laws and punishments were inscribed on human-scaled stone slabs called a stele. One of the most well known of these is the Code of Hammurabi in Babylon, 1792–1750 BCE featuring a carving of King Hammurabi and the sun god Shamash with inscribed writing below.

Graphic design historians feature such objects, but are rightly concerned with the development of what is loosely called writing and pictures, either as an integrated composition, or independently. Issues of importance are attached to the first combined use of 'words and pictures' within the same plane, suggested as the early *Sumerian Blau* monument dated the fourth millennium BCE (Meggs and Purvis 2006: 8). Early multi-lingual communications highlight the use of different writing systems on the same surface, for example the Rosetta Stone, circa 197–196 BCE, with its clear division between hieroglyphic, demotic and Greek inscription. As is the case with the Rosetta Stone, it is often unclear which objects are for public or private consumption, and which were displayed outside or inside buildings.

One particular object emphasized for its multiple purpose is the cylinder seal, not only for longevity and use for 3,000 years but also its role in bringing together image and identity as well communicating a warning (Meggs and Purvis 2006: 9–10). The cylinder seal, when rolled over a slab of damp clay created a repeat impression and acted as an endorsement of quality. Often worn around the neck or wrist, its relevance here is that, as well as a sign of authenticity, it was used to seal a house door when its occupants were away, thus seeking to dissuade potential burglars (a broken seal signalled intrusion).

These examples from the early stages of urban development show different forms of urban inscription. But, property markers, Egyptian obelisks, reliefs and structures that featured in temple architecture are mainly overlooked by graphic design historians as they shift their focus towards papyrus and parchment, and then to the development of alphabets, Chinese calligraphy, illuminated manuscripts, printing and the Middle Ages. A more expansive approach is taken by scholars working specifically in the field of alphabets, hieroglyphs and pictograms, who have researched into how hieroglyphs in architecture were developed by the ancient Maya of Central America.

As Mesopotamian civilization changed in the sixth century BCE under the influence of Persian, then Greco-Roman rule, the interest of graphic design historians in examples of urban graphic objects wanes, the exception being Jubert's reference to Greco-Roman public inscriptions. As well as being painted directly onto the walls of buildings, inscriptions also appeared on swivelling wooden panels – *axons* – used for official pronouncements, publicity advertisements, public games and sporting events. These continue through to the Roman Empire as *alba*, carrying information about 'laws or regulations, political information, electoral "posters", programs of cultural events (festivals, circuses etc.), as well as messages from private individuals to others (such as an appeal for the recapture of an escaped slave, or advertising a horse sale)' (Jubert [2005] 2006: 24).

Evidence from this period is preserved in Pompeii, often cited for its more than 1,600 surviving examples of 'wall writing', as hand-painted lettering displayed at street level on the buildings, often in red for emphasis, both sophisticated and crude in content. See Figure 3.4

After this, graphic design historians do not refer again to the urban interface until the twentieth century. Jubert progresses from showing electoral posters from Pompeii before 79 BCE to handwritten books in the Middle Ages such as *The Book of Kells*, circa 800 CE, early printing in China and, around the same time, manuscripts between 1200–1500 CE, and then printing in Europe leading up to the Guttenberg 42-line Bible between 1452–55 CE. Typography and printing then dominate the analysis until modernity asserts itself in the form of lettering and logotypes inscribed into the building facades of the turbine factory for AEG (Allgemeine Elektrizitäts-Gesellschaft) in 1909 CE. From the same period, the visual identity for London Underground and the later development of posters and maps are highlighted, but it is not until signage design for Roissy-Charles de Gaulle airport, Paris, in 1970–71 CE that anything resembling interface with the built environment as three-dimensional physical objects

FIGURE 3.4 *Wall writing in Pompeii (Pompeii, Italy 2010).*

Three surviving examples of the hand-lettered wall writing also used on wooden panels for information and promotional purposes.

emerges, and only then in discussion about the design of 'a typeface suited to the function and architecture of the airport' (Jubert [2005] 2006: 349). These are shown alongside other examples of signs designed for the Paris Metro. The only other example to feature is the signage for British roads in the early 1960s, before interest surfaces in the final decades of the twentieth century. Jubert then concentrates on examples of typography used in signage for transport infrastructure, building façade restoration with light box lettering, environmental application of new signage for the Dutch post office in 1988–89, and Joan Brossa's (1909–1999) 'Visual-Walkable-Poem in Three Parts' at the Velòdrom d'Horta, Barcelona from 1984. But there is no attempt to contextualize these from a built environmental perspective.

Jubert gives a glimpse of the art nouveau station entrances to the Paris Métro in a rare 1903 photograph, and an elevation drawing of the same scheme from 1900, but these serve only to support printed items such as posters, pamphlet covers and book binding, and escape mention in the main text ([2005] 2006: 115). Furthermore, a colour scheme and layout for the De Unie café in Rotterdam, 1925, in the style of De Stijl is shown but not explained ([2005] 2006: 190), as is Herbert Bayer's (1900–1985) design for a cigarette kiosk featuring an illuminated P sign, as part of a wider discussion about the Bauhaus ([2005] 2006: 202). Bayer's work in this area is also featured by Meggs and Purvis (2006: 316) in a design for a streetcar station and newsstand combining waiting area and newsstand with rooftop advertising panels.

By comparison, after Meggs and Purvis highlight Trajan's Column and wall-writing in Pompeii, no urban artefacts of relevance deserve their attention until the same examples from AEG and London Underground, and their respective company 'symbols' within a context referred to as corporate design. The design for Café de Unie is merited for the harmonious integration of architectural and graphic forms. Signage for the 1968 Olympic Games in Mexico City as well as the 1984 Olympics in Los Angeles demonstrates an integration between street furniture and environmental signage.

In these significant studies of graphic design's history, the urban setting is barely recognized as a context for graphic design. Yet history is present in accounts of graphic design work. For example, influential designers such as Peter Behrens (1868–1940) and Edward Johnston (1872–1944) are acknowledged as being predisposed to the art and design of ancient Greece and Rome. In the case of AEG in Germany, Behrens understood the 'formal language of harmony and proportion needed to achieve a unity of the parts of the whole', explicit in his typeface designs based on the proportions of Roman inscription lettering (Meggs and Purvis 2006: 233–43). Specifically, in his design for the *Behrens-Antiqua* font he strove for 'a monumental character that could evoke positive connotations of quality and performance'. Illustrating Behrens's corporate design programme, Meggs and Purvis show the application of lettering to storefronts, contrasting in scale with the Turbine Hall example shown by Jubert. In the case of the London Underground, Meggs and Purvis pay homage to Johnston's station signage and symbol for what was then known as the Electric Railways Company of London (UERL), including his new sans-serif typeface influenced by the proportions of classical

Roman inscription. In designing the Underground Railways Sans typeface – invariably known as 'Johnston's Railway Type' (Meggs and Purvis 2006: 242), 'Underground, Johnston, Johnston Underground, Railway Type, or Railway' (Jubert [2005] 2006: 234) or 'Underground Railway' (Lussu 2001: 100) – Johnston responded to a brief for a typeface that combined the 'bold simplicity shown by distinctive letters from preceding epochs, but with an undisputably twentieth-century quality' (Meggs and Purvis 2006: 243). Johnston achieved this by drawing on his knowledge of Roman square capital letters detailed in his book *Writing & Illuminating & Lettering* ([1906] 1977: 232–300) a decade or so earlier. This will be further discussed soon.

In sum, graphic design's urban history gives importance to the development of writing as part of the ancient city's cultivating influence, but the graphic-urban interface is then neglected for two millennia except for a few examples of graphic design applied to the development of transport infrastructure and corporate identity. Yet graphic design is proffered as being part of the urban fabric, as noted in Chapter 1. But in graphic design's urban history there is simply not enough explanation about what this means, why it matters and how it happens. The following case studies show how some basic principles in the design of letterforms have survived hundreds of years and are engrained on our minds.

Trajan's Column, Rome

The Forum of Trajan was one of imperial Rome's most important complexes for culture, commerce and communication; a vast monument to the achievements of the emperor Trajan and his army, displaying an omnipresent use of military imagery. Born in 53 CE, Trajan ruled from 98 CE until his death in 117 CE. Planned and built by the military engineer and architect Apollodorus of Damascus between 106–13 CE, the forum was accessed through an arch to the south-east into a market place containing an equestrian statue of Trajan. On the other side of the market place stood the Basilica Ulpia law court, located axially across the full width of the complex. Like the public squares in Mesopotamia, the forum provided a place to post new laws. Beyond this is sited Trajan's Column in a courtyard flanked by the Biblotheca Ulpia Greek library to the north-east and Latin library to the south-west. Directly opposite – completed later in 128 CE by Hadrian – the Temple of Trajan occupied the north-west border.

The column is the best-preserved structure from the forum, which functioned for several centuries until being destroyed during an earthquake in 801 CE. As well as celebrating the spoils of war, the column pedestal accommodates Trajan's ashes in a small burial chamber. It is best known for its helical frieze that spirals from bottom to top of a tapered shaft, the highly detailed sculptured imagery depicting an historical account as events unfolded of two Dacian wars. Conveyed in a 200-metre spiralling band that varies in height between 77 and 145 centimetres deep, it is a continuously illustrated pictorial scroll cut into the column surface, the narrative detailing Trajan's success. Topped originally with a bronze statue of the emperor, the column stands 35.07 metres high to the top of the statue base and is built from 29 blocks of Luna marble, with 185 inside steps spiralling up to a square balcony that accommodates 12 people. See Plate 2.

Visiting the column now as a single-standing monument raises questions about how such detailed relief sculptured images could be fully appreciated. An understanding of the architectural setting provides answers as to how the column was 'read.' Situated in a 25 × 18 metre paved court immediately surrounded by colonnades on three sides and a wall on the fourth side of the basilica, architectural reconstructions support the idea that porticos on three sides had flat accessible roofs, with a viewing gallery on the Basilica side providing a fourth perspective (Coulston 1988: 13–14). This is speculated to have provided views of the top from 8 metres at an angle of 45° at a portico height of 11 metres, or 13 metres from the adjacent Basilica. The frieze started at 9 metres up from the courtyard from which the top of the spiral could be seen at a 70° angle. It has also been suggested that public viewing arrangements were envisaged by the planners and sculptors for select audiences because, beyond the forum, views of the column were restricted from all but the north-west side. However, the exact layout of the courtyard (and Trajan's Temple) varies in different plans of the forum complex, as do overall plans of the forum, some showing the entrance arch as part of a curved front whilst others show it as perpendicular.

Even though Trajan's Column is best known for its helical frieze, it is also acclaimed for the monumental inscription above the entrance door in the column pedestal, as previously noted. Completed after the sculpting of the relief frieze due to the scaffolding covering the pedestal, the inscription dedicates the monument in 113 CE but is otherwise not connected to the frieze above in terms of content.

Edward Johnston's analysis of the inscription confirms the dimensions of the stone (3 feet 9 inches high by 9 feet and ¾ inches), the surrounding border (4 inches), the letters (approximate heights: first two lines are 4½ inches, second two lines 4⅜ inches, fifth line 4⅛ inches and the last line 3⅞ inches), and the spaces between the lines decreasing from 3 to 2¾ inches ([1906] 1977: 371–73). The inscription lettering descends in size as it is read from top to bottom and possible reasons given by Johnston vary: the top of the inscription is further away from the reader and therefore should be larger; large headings are more architecturally beautiful; and inscription beginnings are often larger for emphasis and importance. Although the inscription did not include H, J, K, U, W, Y, and Z, Johnston ([1906] 1977: 233) divided the proportions of Roman letter width in two, as wide or narrow. Wide letters were either 'round' (O Q C G D) or 'square' (M W H (U) A N V T (Z)) (though none were exactly square, some being slightly narrower), and narrow letters (B E F R S Y (X) I J K L P) more conformist, this situating X as a narrow letter. This analysis by Johnson unknowingly treats the inscription as a composite graphic object in a graphic space, with a subset of graphic objects as letterforms that are each divided into sets. More recent analysis of Roman letterforms, based on rubbings and line drawings of the Trajan's Column inscription has been compared with the Roman inscription for

FIGURE 3.5 *Inscription at the base of Trajan's Column in Rome (London, UK 2014 from a cast in the Victoria & Albert Museum).*

Viewed from three metres away looking upward, the descending size of letters from top to bottom is clearly displayed.

The Memorial to the Children of Freedon Sextus Pompeius on Appian Way in Rome (dated from the first or second century CE). The comparison reveals a proportioning system based on sacred geometry used by the Egyptians and the Greeks in architecture and the design of artefacts, providing the basic structure for Roman capitals (Perkins 2000: 35–51).

The suggestion is that for inscriptions as important as Trajan's Column, a system was used for the preliminary marking out of an inscription before 'brushing in' the letters that guide the inscription-carving process. 'Most of the great monumental inscriptions were designed in situ by a master writer, and only cut in by the mason, the cutting being merely a fixing, as it were, of the writing, and the cut inscriptions must always have been intended to be completed by painting' (Lethaby [1906] 1977: xiii). Not all of the Trajan inscription letters fit exactly within a geometric framework due to the imperfection of freehand writing, but a method for proportioning the letters at different scales offers a plausible explanation as to why inscriptions appear as they do, following a sacred tradition found in the art of Egypt, India, China, Islam and other traditional civilizations (Perkins 2000: 36). Figure 3.6 indicates how the proportions of

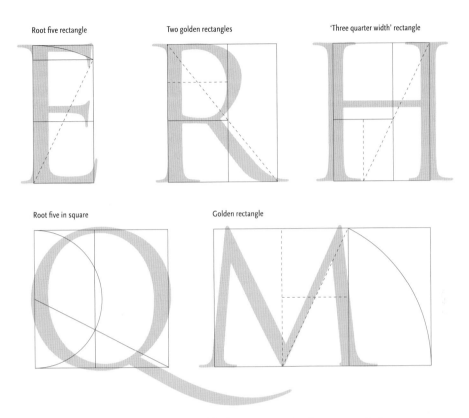

FIGURE 3.6 *Five basic geometric models for constructing Roman capitals.*
By superimposing the modern Trajan *typeface derived from the Trajan's Column inscription onto an underlying grid based on the root five and golden rectangles, the proportioning system used by master writers is apparent.*

Roman capital letters align with what Perkins (2000: 35) explains as the 'root five' rectangle and the 'Golden Rectangle' derived from the Golden Mean.

Two thousand years on, the column inscription provides a robust example of urban inscription and public proclamation in imperial Rome. Its relevance is evident in the way Johnston's Underground Railways Sans' letter O is circular and fits into a square, as does the M, Q, and X and the 'thin, double square' E, though it is not quite as narrow as a root five rectangle. The lettering's geometric structure replicates a practice and established an aesthetic and legible standard against which future typeface designs have been compared.

The Roman Alphabet is the foundation of our alphabets. . . . And since the full development of their monumental forms about 2000 years ago, the Roman Capitals have held the supreme place among letters for readableness and beauty. They are the best forms for the grandest and most important inscriptions and, in regard to lettering generally, a very good rule to follow is: *When in doubt, use Roman Capitals*.

JOHNSTON [1906] 1977: 232, original italics

The Trajan's Column inscription clearly influenced the design of lettering as it evolved in the late nineteenth century, and although first used in 1916–17, Johnston's *Underground Railways Sans* typeface and later *Gill Sans* by Eric Gill provide two examples. More recently, its updated and digitized form called *New Johnston TfL* continues to be used by *Transport for London*, with its versatility and association with London extending to the wayfinding signage for London's 2012 Olympic Games (Lucas 2013: 26–8). However, the helical frieze wrapping around the column shaft from bottom to top, for which it is best-known, has beem overlooked by graphic design historians. It was clearly a spectacle and of significant historic importance. As the most written about Roman monument and artwork the frieze is said to 'graphically' provide historical commentary for the emperor's reign more than any literary evidence (Coulston 1988: 2).

Johnston's 'Underground' typeface

When in the early twentieth century Frank Pick – the commercial manager for the Electric Railways Company of London (now London Underground) – began thinking about how to unify the different parts of the tube network through its visual identity, his first instinct was the classical Trajan style lettering already in use on the station platform bookstalls. Instead, he opted for something contrasting, and commissioned Edward Johnston's 1916 humanist sans serif typeface design that remains in use a century later and is applied to all signs, maps and publicity materials. It has been the standard for all London Transport graphic communication, from trains and buses to bicycles, having spawned updated versions for phototypesetting in 1979 and then for digitization in 2002 (both using a revised design called *New Johnston* by Eiichi Kono).

The typeface's defining properties derive from simple geometric form, consistent stroke weight and quirky detail derived from Johnston's expert knowledge of calligraphy. This is most evident in the original diamond shaped dot over the miniscule letters i and j, and also more recently in Kono's version which extends this quirk to the apostrophe and comma. Used recently for wayfinding at the 2012 Olympic Games, these subtle details are a small connection between the event branding and London's more extensive environmental graphic image (see Plate 3).

To be more exact, Johnston received the commission in 1913 to create a typeface with clarity and distinction. This was soon implemented across the network communications as part of a period of architectural and design unification between 1916 and 1929. It first appeared publicly on posters for tram fares in 1917, and soon after on signs and was integrated into the London Underground diagram (or London

PLATE 1 *An assortment of urban objects (Delft, The Netherlands 2011; Tokyo, Japan 2013; Oslo, Norway 2013; London, UK 2010; Rome, Italy 2009; San Francisco, USA 2013; Gothenberg, Sweden 2013; Dubai, United Arab Emirates 2009; Paris, France 2015; Philadelphia, USA 2014; Seoul, South Korea 2009; Montreal, Canada 2010; São Paulo, Brazil 2010; London, UK 2015; New York, USA 2010; Latina, Italy 2015; Market Harborough, UK 2015; Oslo, Norway 2013).*

Urban designers do not categorize these much beyond a miscellaneous group of things.

LIVERPOOL JOHN MOORES UNIVERSITY
LEARNING SERVICES

PLATE 2 *Trajan's Column (Rome, Italy 2009).*
Best known for its helical frieze, it is also celebrated for the inscription at the base, a model for the design of Roman typefaces.

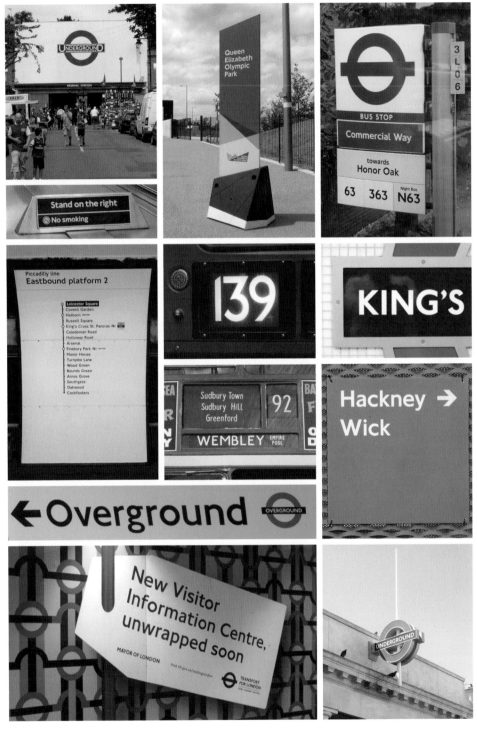

PLATE 3 *A variety of Transport for London graphic elements (London, UK 2010–2015).*
The system is underpinned by the consistent application of Edward Johnston's 'Underground'
typeface design.

PLATE 4 *Connect Sheffield pedestrian signage system (Sheffield, England 2008).*
The full type–typographic–graphic–urban design spectrum is on view here.

PLATE 5 *Empire State Building (New York, USA 2010 and 2014).*
The building's silhouette and façade lettering both stand out from their immediate surroundings.

PLATE 6 *Shinjuku's Skyscraper District (Tokyo, Japan 2013).*

From the ground upwards, surfaces display an array of graphic objects serving different functions, designed to stand out from an otherwise subdued grey cityscape.

PLATE 7 *Shinjuku's Kabukichō district (Tokyo, Japan 2013).*

The Studio Alta façade greets pedestrians as they leave Shinjuku Station through the East exit. A landmark and node, it is a popular meeting place before heading further into Kabukichō. Beyond this point Tokyo's largest red light district is saturated in a medley of graphic choices from the 'torii' (gate) to the Hanazono-jinja temple.

PLATE 8 *Shinjuku's urban fabric (Tokyo, Japan 2013).*

Throughout, graphic elements adorn and enhance Shinjuku's urban infrastructure in relatively permanent and performative ways.

PLATE 9 *City of Westminster street nameplate (London, Market Harborough, Llandudno, Lutterworth and Oxford, UK 2013–2015).*

The sign's modernist aesthetic, derived from the 'new-typography' compared to that of 'old typography', is now much copied for its simple aspirational appeal. Its appropriated meanings are increasingly used in popular culture.

PLATE 10 *Permanent and semi-permanent graphic messages (Longano, Italy 2006; Blackpool, UK 2014; São Paulo, Brazil 2010; Market Harborough, UK 2013 and 2012; Seoul, South Korea 2009; Tiverton, UK 2007).*

Carpets, illuminations, protective clothing, warning tape, guidelines, and topiary, defy the media specificity of urban graphic objects.

PLATE 11 *The importance of architectural integrity (Rome, Italy 2009).*

Heritage considerations add to the ensemble that determines the discreet form of this McDonald's fascia in Rome's Piazza di Spagna. Although the familiar McDonald's lettering is scaled to fill the available space, the sympathetic fascia colour fits with the local vernacular, unlike the city's Metro sign.

PLATE 12 *A floorscape of colonial memory (top; Lisbon, Portugal 2006: bottom; São Paulo, Brazil 2010, 2012, 2014).*

The patterned floorscape of Lisbon and São Paulo represents the historical link and spatial relations between Portugal and Brazil, spanning more than 500 years.

PLATE 13 *Ghirardelli Square, San Francisco (San Francisco, USA 2013).*

At this historically significant location, graphic objects add a layer of communication to the architecture, facilitating and redefining human interaction with place in time and space.

PLATE 14 *La Défence, Hauts-de-Seine (Hauts-de-Seine, France 2015).*

La Défence is a predominantly grey place where graphic objects provide highlights, defining the form of most things that are not traditionally architecture or landscape architecture.

PLATE 15 *Theater District and Times Square (New York, USA 2010 and 2014).*

Not so much a square but a crossroads, this popular tourist destination displays much more than the electronic advertising panels that cover every available façade. It functions through many forms of graphic address.

PLATE 16 COOPAMARE (São Paulo, Brazil 2010 and 2014).

The Cooperative of Autonomous Paper, Cardboard, Scraps and Reusable Materials Collectors (COOPAMARE) is located under a viaduct in the Pinheiros area of São Paulo. Much to the distress of local residents, co-operative workers service the city after decades of transformation from homeless people to citizens of the city.

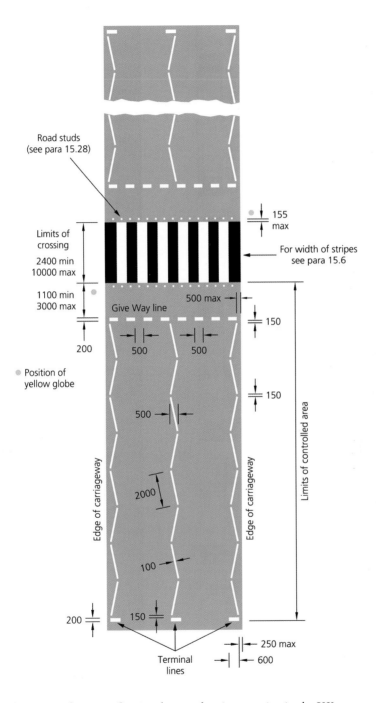

PLATE 17 *Zebra: specification for a pedestrian crossing in the UK.*

The implementation of a 'zebra' crossing in the UK conforms with this basic configuration.

PLATE 18 *Zebra: the elementary components of a zebra crossing (Market Harborough and Blackpool, UK 2015).*

The crossing is comprised of painted parallel rectangles at the point of crossing, give way and diagonal lines, amber globe lamp (or Belisha beacon) mounted on poles, and road studs. These combine to warn the motorist of pedestrians crossing as well as signify to the pedestrian a safe place to cross.

PLATE 19 *Zebra: overhead graphic device (São Paulo, Brazil 2014).*

Beyond the UK, additional overhead devices signal to the driver the likelihood of a pedestrian crossing the road below.

PLATE 20 *Zebra: adaptations to the basic pedestrian crossing pattern (Tokyo, Japan 2013; São Paulo, Brazil 2012; Valencia, Spain 2014; Paris, France 2015).*

The basic black and white parallel lines of the zebra crossing have been adapted to completely cover junctions, provide plenty of width to cope with high pedestrian numbers, and bend and angle around corners.

PLATE 21 *Zebra: urban and rural application (New York, USA 2010; Oslo, Norway 2013; Longano, Italy 2009).*

Across the urban–rural continuum, painted stripes indicate to the pedestrian a place to cross, even where there is no sidewalk!

PLATE 22 *Zebra: durability, permanence and prestige (Delft, The Netherlands 2011; Umeå, Sweden 2014; Oslo, Norway 2013; Boras, Sweden 2013; and again Boras, Sweden 2013; Lisbon, Portugal 2006; Paris, France 2015; Leeds, UK 2014).*

Hard floorscaping utilizes the basic white stripes to establish a permanence in some of the most prestigious city streets such as the Avenue des Champs-Élysées in Paris.

PLATE 23 *Zebra: view from the Arc de Triomphe (Paris, France 2015).*

A plan view of the Arc de Triomphe reveals three concentric circles of road markings circumnavigating the monument across all of its 12 converging avenues.

PLATE 24 *Zebra: variations in colour (Isernia, Italy 2014; Rome, Italy 2015).*

These versions in Italy incorporate an additional colour to further identify the crossing. The vibrancy of the top image (the photograph is not retouched) is due to repainting in anticipation of the Pope's 2014 visit to the city.

PLATE 25 *Zebra: floor colour (Seoul, South Korea 2009).*

Although white stripes may be used with other coloured floor surfacinq, there is no guarantee of pedestrian compliance.

PLATE 26 *Zebra: integration with landscape (Tokyo, Japan 2013; London, UK 2014; Valencia, Spain 2014; Blackpool, UK 2014).*

In these examples, the purity of the crossing fits the geometry of the landscaping within which it functions.

PLATE 27 *Zebra: incorporating writing systems (Hong Kong 2007).*

This colour co-ordinated crossing, matching the amber globes, demonstrates how the stripes work with two additional language variations.

LIVERPOOL JOHN MOORES UNIVERSITY
LEARNING SERVICES

PLATE 28 *Zebra: continuity of pattern (Lisbon, Portugal 2006).*

A consistent patterning device may enhance the transition from sidewalk to carriageway in historically sensitive areas.

PLATE 29 *Zebra: a safe and secure place to cross (London Stansted, UK 2007).*

Some environments, especially those unfamiliar to us such as an airport, require that we are more alert to safety and security matters when making short journeys by foot.

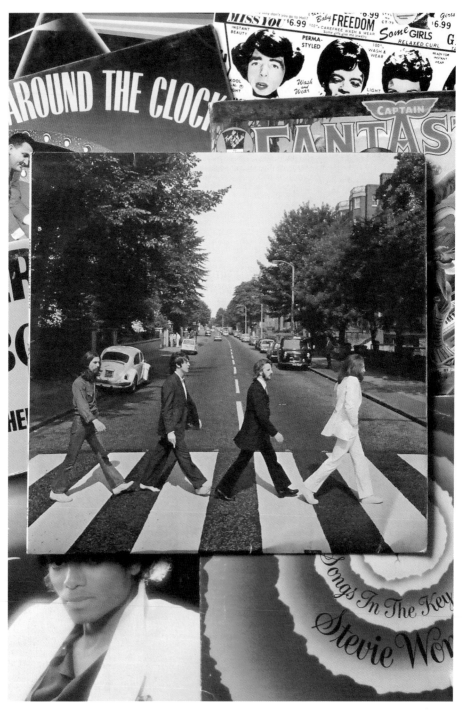

PLATE 30 *Zebra: the Beatles* Abbey Road *album cover.*

Based on an initial sketch by Paul McCartney, this cover image is now a tourist attraction for generations of Beatles fans.

PLATE 31 *Zebra: Shibuya Crossing (Tokyo, Japan 2013).*

Every few minutes, Tokyo's Shibuya Crossing stages a scramble to get to the other side, with constraining lines doing little to maintain order.

PLATE 32 *Zebra: activism (Market Harborough, UK 2013).*

At this dangerous place to cross, pedestrians are at risk from vehicles turning into the crossing with the driver unsighted. A member of the public painted white lines on the carriageway, but these were painted out soon after by the local council.

Underground map) in 1933, soon after Henry Beck conceived the diagram. Since then it has been an integral part of the transport network in London and consequently it is referred to as 'London's letterform', acknowledging its contribution to the city's identity. It is said to be 'one of the most iconic, enduring and best-loved fonts in the world' (Garfield 2010: 114).

This detail in London's urban landscape is relatively unacknowledged in urban design. Yet its relationship to contemporary urban design is ever present. For example, the Jubilee Line extension underground rail link in London is defined as an example of 'plug-in urban design' (Lang 2005: 334–338), but the typeface is overlooked. Yet it is implicitly part of London Underground's visually unifying signage and extended set of graphic elements that includes the roundel, colour scheme, pictograms and complete wayfinding system as part of Transport for London's consolidated environmental information system.

Emergent 'environmental information systems'

The growth of cities since the 1950s has coincided with increased interest in 'information' in the built environment, but at nowhere near an equivalent pace. Nevertheless, in the late 1940s, interest emerged in the need for clear information for public transport systems, under the guise of good design. In the UK, the emergence of design as a profession in the post-war years resulted in greater focus on the kind of urban objects of interest to us here. For example, *Design*, the monthly journal for manufacturers and designers, featured an article on 'signpost design' (Tomrley 1950) soon after the magazine launched. This featured work by the Ministry of Works Chief Architects' Department, which was responsible for signing many buildings in the UK ranging from palaces to shelters. The article is an early example of public interest in the standard of lettering on public signs, and brings to light debate in the Cambridge Town Council and discussion in the *Cambridge Daily News* about the appearance of new street nameplates which led to protests against the shape and spacing of sans-serif capital letters. It emphasized not only the need for better standards of inscriptional lettering, but also the introduction of a systematic approach to letter spacing that could be implemented by untrained operatives to enhance the legibility of signs seen obliquely.

Further articles appeared in *Design* throughout 1950 in various numbered issues. Number 19 featured 'van lettering as part of a consistent Design Policy'. Later that year, number 21 included an article about heating engineers standardizing the design for painted, printed and engraved lettering on their contractor's signboards, as well as a small article on the *Notebook* page about the use of Egyptian lettering on shop and inn signs in the East and North Midlands. The *Notebook* page in number 22 also recognized praise given to the bus-stop signs for London Transport in publications such as *Transport World* (January 1944), *Architects Journal* (March 1944) and *Art & Industry* (October

1946). *Design* focussed on the London Transport roundel symbol with BUS STOP centred in the cross bar. It is described as 'a frameless folded sheet of enamelled iron, mounted on a concrete post (with a jaunty red metal tip for its finial) which incorporates a panel for timetables on the side facing the pavement' (Anon 1950: 32). The London Transport roundel features again in an article in number 31 (Carrington and Harris 1951). Furthermore, in an article *Legibility or 'architectural appropriateness'?* Noel Carrington (1951: 27–9) is critical of the use of Egyptian lettering for the Festival of Britain and uses several illustrations to demonstrate that sign posting is not large enough, lettering against a 'dazzle backgound' makes for slow reading, concern about the small scale application of lettering, and problems with shadow on relief lettering. By 1954, number 69 introduced the idea that a design issue as small as the choice of lettering, or the inter-character spacing of letters, is synthesized into a the wider discussion about street furniture (Williams 1954). The article begins as follows:

> Visit practically any city, town or village in the British Isles and you will find evidence of the bad design and careless siting of street furniture. Look at the main street in some of the larger cities and you will find an appalling muddle of objects. This haphazard sprouting has even outpaced the rapid growth of road transport and other forms of communication, leaving a surfeit in conflicting shapes, sizes, styles and colours. Much of it defeats the primary object and leads to the confusion of road users and pedestrians alike.
>
> ibid: 15–16

The article talks about a multiplicity of objects that include 'street lighting', 'traffic signs', 'street name-plates and numbers', 'postal pillar-boxes', 'signals', 'guard rails', 'telephone and police boxes', 'beacons', 'electrical transmission poles', 'bollards', 'seats', 'litter baskets and bins', and 'fire alarm posts'.

Since this recognition of a particular type of design in the urban environment, there has been intermittent interest in the graphic elements of the built environment. This is evidenced in a periodic succession of books with lettering at their core, the first of which claims to be *Lettering on Buildings* (Gray 1960) followed by *Lettering in Architecture* (Bartram 1975), *Fascia Lettering in the British Isles* (1978a), *Street Name Lettering in the British Isles* (1978b), *Words and Buildings: the Art and Practice of Public Lettering* (1980), and *Signs: Lettering in the Environment* (Baines and Dixon 2003), to name some of the better known. Throughout this period, other publications evidence the scope and variety of signs. *Signs in Action* (Sutton 1965) also includes symbols as hanging signs, assorted hand-painted signs, hand-drawn price tickets on market stalls, neon signs that are pictorial as well as word based. This is strongly influenced by material featured in Herbert Spencer's magazine *Typographica* (1949–1967) which, in 1963, drew attention to such mundane objects as manhole covers. Spencer featured a photograph of the façade for Bar Toto in Rome which is described as 'both palimpsest and collage, as successive modes of communication overlay but never entirely obliterate earlier styles of graphic address: stone-carved lettering, graffiti, post box, advertising, neon sign' (Poyner 2002: 70).

Some publications are quirkier. For example: *Graphicswallah* (Lovegrove 2003) features hand-painted murals and advertisements in India; *Paris Underground* (Archer and Parré 2005) documents 300 years of paintings, drawings, graffiti and sculpture on the walls of 177 miles of man-made tunnels under the streets of Paris; *Sign Language: Street Signs as Folk Art* (Baeder 1996) is a collection of handmade street signs in America portrayed as folk art; and *Letters on America: photographs and lettering* (Fella 2000) features 1134 Polaroid photographs. Furthermore, *Nowhere in Particular* (Miller 1999) is an esoteric portrayal of decaying facades where lettering has been removed which has left a residue of erosion to discolour a surface, but which also leaves a trace of a letterform as well as torn billboard posters. This is reminiscent of work by French artists Raymond Haines and Jacques Villeglé in the 1950s (Anon 1999). More geographically specific and politically motivated is *The Writings on the Wall: Peace at the Berlin Wall* (Tillman 1990) featuring images of graffiti on the Berlin Wall, in a book about freedom. The list goes on and graphic images of signs in the built environment are increasingly available from many perspectives.

Built environment professionals also use photographic images to explain their interest in managing the environment. *City Signs and Lights* (Carr 1973) is a study into the chaotic array of public and private signs and lights in the city of Boston and attempts to assist in the planning and legibility of the city through better understanding 'environmental information systems'. This employs the use of graphic design consultancy and features Kevin Lynch as an urban design consultant (we further discuss Lynch in Chapter 4) in what is probably one of the earliest examples of graphic design and urban design contributing to city planning. Not until the early 1990s do the these disciplines unite again with any significance in *Wayfinding: people, signs and architecture* (Arthur and Passini [1992] 2002), the first notable attempt to elaborate on Lynch's ideas about 'way-finding' from the early 1960s. Wayfinding has since become a focus of attention, and in *Wayfinding: designing and implementing graphic navigational systems* (Berger 2005) the phrase 'environmental graphic design' is used to describe a new specialism. This is said to represent the merging of graphic design and architecture with the assistance of fields such as industrial design and urban planning.

Building on this new direction, *Wayshowing: A Guide to Environmental Signage Principles and Practices* (Mollerup 2005) introduces a number of principles that are applied to a range of contexts including hospitals, airports, rails, museums and cities by discussing:

- the difference between wayfinding and wayshowing;

- practical theory about why many signs do not work;

- the function of signs as identification, direction, description and regulation;

- the importance of toponomy (the discipline of giving names);

- sign content as typography, pictograms, arrows, guidelines, and maps;

- sign form as colour, size, format, grids and groupings;

- location, mounting and lighting;

- inclusive design, (especially visual impairment and means); and

- the importance of planning and its processes, and branding.

Finally, *The Works: Anatomy of the City* (Ascher [2005] 2007) offers a contemporary overview of how twenty-first century New York works through its urban graphic objects. This comprises of: traffic signals and traffic cameras; traffic calming measures; the art of manhole covers; street markings for street repair; street signs; parking meters; the letter system of subway names and the use of tokens between 1910 and the 1990s; subway system signals; steam vents; fire alarm boxes; and policing. New York provides a snapshot of how a modern city works through the array of miscellaneous urban graphic objects on display. The scale is staggering. Nearly 20,000 miles of streets and highways connect New York's five boroughs, with 40,000 intersections of which 11,400 are governed by traffic lights, not to mention more than 1 million street signs adorning the city's roads (Ascher 2005: 2–21). Human interaction with this aspect of the city is characterized by parking rules and restrictions, a pedestrian crossing system, one-way traffic patterns, bus lanes, track routes, 'thru streets', and limited-access roads. All of these carry some form of graphic address, at its most intense in Times Square where environmental information systems are dense.

Although graphic design's history books do not fully acknowledge the extent of a relationship between graphic form and urban context, various magazines and trade journals such as the quarterly *Eye Magazine*, the monthly *Creative Review* and the International Society of Typographic Designers' journal *Typographic*, regularly do in ways that underpin the type–typographic–graphic–urban relationship introduced in Chapter 1. For example, in March 2013, *Creative Review* (March 2013) published a special issue on London Underground as a 150-year review of their visual communications. This traced the evolution of commercial art and advertising during the first 50 years, through to the tube map, Edward Johnston's typeface (as noted above) and its subsequent use in the Underground roundel symbol, posters that promoted tube travel, large scale public art and the licensing, merchandising and development of the brand. From a public realm perspective, *Eye Magazine* (issue 34) published a special issue exploring signage, culture and civic projects that integrate form, content and media through graphic elements, the enduring influence of *Learning from Las Vegas* (Venturi *et al.* 1977) and commercial art in the public realm such as the effervescence of neon, tart cards, out-of-town shopping and the role of photography as a medium for creating images of the city streets. In particular, the attention given to *Learning from Las Vegas* reiterated its emphasis on image, symbolic and representational elements as more important than form, position and orientation (Heathcote 1999: 46–

8), but its focus on commercial contexts limits an appreciation of the wider functions of individual graphic objects.

On a more specific note, type design features in explanations about how each of Amsterdam's 2000 bridges were named and labelled with cast steel letters in the 1930s, using the bespoke Amsterdam Bridge Type (Amsterdamse Brugletter) (Middendorp 2008). On a more critical note, questions such as why Mistral is the typeface of choice for so many of Montreal's small businesses are answered (Soar 2004: 50–7). Furthermore, discussion about the creation of a photographic archive of Lisbon's lettering in the Central Lettering Record at Central Saint Martins at the University of the Arts London extends the work of earlier lettering historians from the 1960s (Baines and Dixon 2004: 26–35). All emphasize an infatuation with lettering that overlaps directly with architectural interests. But that is not all.

These few examples emphasize the intertwined nature of lettering and type design (meaning the design of typefaces), but these are two distinct, if closely related, activities. Baines and Dixon (2002: 8–9) suggest lettering is concerned with letterforms – the alphabetic symbols developed over thousands of years – and is the 'parent discipline' of type design, but with greater capacity for scope between utility, creativity and responsiveness to local context. Amsterdam Bridge Type and Mistral are type designs, whereas Baines and Dixon argue that lettering does not concern itself with industrial production in the way type design does. The implication for the way this distinction is understood in this book is that the author's perspective is framed more by an understanding of type design than lettering, but through type design access is clearly granted to the realm of lettering to supplement the main argument and emphasize design as a common link between type–typographic–graphic–urban design.

In the same way that lettering and type design are closely related, and clearly feed into typographic design, a relationship between type design, typographic design and graphic design is implicit in studies that show a wider context for type design that also extends to the level of city council involvement. One of these is the Sheffield City Council initiative to develop pedestrian signage and mapping for on-street, online and print applications in their Connect Sheffield initiative, crossing the full spectrum of type–typographic–graphic–urban design activity. At the smallest detail a new font, Sheffield Sans was designed by type designer Jeremy Tankard as part of a scheme devised by graphic design practice Atelier Works (Baines and Dixon 2005). See Plate 4. This scheme synthesises graphic representation into clearly defined graphic spaces as urban structures. Each contains a variable set of sub-graphic objects in the form bespoke typographic, photographic, diagrammatic, pictographic and ideographic exemplifications, and a clock face. These composite graphic structures convey local content and also utilise graphic devices that link to wider networks, such as the British Rail symbol.

Furthermore, typographic design featured prominently in the previously shown Comedy Carpet in Figure 1.4, where visual research undertaken for the project benefited from archived comedy posters displaying a medley of typographic designs (Lucas 2011: 42).

These contrasting examples emphasize the role of graphic design at an interface with urban design. But they are intermittent, as are revelries about ideas that have changed graphic design. These are varied and include the impact of 'monumental graphics' associated with European Fascism in the 1930s, 'supergraphics' appearing on the outside of buildings as complete facades, 'light spectaculars' typical of those seen in Las Vegas and in the way modern skyscrapers are lit, and 'street slogans' that featured in the 1968 student uprisings in Paris (Heller and Vienne 2012).

What we deduce from this short review is that there is an emergent connection between type–typographic–graphic–urban design practice which is reflected in much of the literature. Typographic discourse has a tradition incorporating a wider graphic design perspective and its scope to incorporate both literate and figurative images. The previously mentioned post-war visual arts publication *Typographica* is one of the best examples of this in how it juxtaposed the 'visual and textual' and championed photography 'as a new form of literacy' (Poyner 1999: 64–73).

Summary

This chapter has further explained what an urban graphic object is, and positioned it as something concrete. It has examined the use of terminology used by urbanists, clarified the meaning of urban and urban design, disclosed graphic design's urban historical perspective from ancient times to the present, reviewed some of the associated literature, and highlighted case studies about Trajan's Column in Rome and Edward Johnston's 'Underground' typeface in London. These two case studies illustrate how urban graphic objects are linked through time and space. With this focus on inscription, this has explained how graphic objects are a detailed part of urban objects. used by

Graphic design's urban history clearly positions the origin of graphic design aligned to the early development of cities in Egypt, Mesopotamia, and the Indus Valley area. This took the form of carved sculptural objects that integrated 'picture' and 'written' representations, a medium still used today amidst the electronic light spectacular advertising displays in New York's Times Square, which is a modern-day version of the painted lettering on walls and swiveling wooden panels in ancient Rome. At this early stage in the relationship between graphic form and urban form, inscription was shown to have evolved as a result of both mental and physical effort, as geometric shapes held in the memory were transferred through the hand and brush to a stone surface. Then, the inscription was carved out and in-filled with paint (a modern version of this process is still in use today, as seen on gravestones). This was often undertaken freehand, but also with much advanced preparation and planning in terms of layout. In this process we see an early example of design process at work, as a conceiving, planning and making activity through shared systematic endeavour, drawing on historical precedents passed down through generations. Today, the making of electronic messages in Times Square is, to some extent, a more elaborate design activity. Whereas a simpler street sign, despite it's mechanical production for most examples seen on street corners, still utilises hand-made novelty on rare occasions.

A gap in the graphic design history literature between antiquity and modernism exposes the poor attention given to the urban by historians working in art and design. This is should not be surprising given that art and design is a relatively recent addition to higher education (as shown in Chapter 2) and is fragmented into a wide range of practices, perhaps united only by the common activity of drawing. Graphic design history's portrayal of the urban context tends to primarily feature examples of lettering and typography, paying scant attention to the massive diversity of messages that adorn the urban environment (a preoccupation of this book). Since the middle of the twentieth century, professional and trade magazines and journals foster discourse that directly links a type–typographic–graphic–urban design continuum, but the urban context mainly forms the backdrop to discussion and is therefore overlooked by historians working in art and design. An exception to this is the way Edward Johnston's typeface design for the consolidated underground railway system is linked to the much larger scale architectural and design work for what became London Underground and is now part of the wider Transport for London network. The ubiquity of Johnston's typeface, and its multi-purpose use on a multiplicity of things, from advertising and information panels to bus numbers and bus stops, has been shown to be an embedded urban design detail and immediate identifier for London. Nowhere else in the world is there such consistency and scale in application of a typeface in an urban environment. It unifies people movement around that city.

In the discussion about how urban is defined, interpretations of the word urban were shown to be universally inconsistent and this is echoed in the varied interpretations of urban design. Definitions of urban design were shown to range from the suggestion it is everything seen from a window to something more about structures, settings and life. It is about complex relationships. Hence, it has been easier to look across the range of settlement types for evidence of how built and unbuilt space functions through graphic objects. This is important because a street sign may be found in a small hamlet or village just as much as a megacity. However, certain graphic objects, such as an interactive building skin will mostly be found in cities of a certain size, and only then in site-specific situations, despite far-fetched claims that responsive environments are ubiquitous.

The design of urban environments is dependent on historical knowledge and understanding from many different sources. A graphic design perspective has been shown to be one of these. Urban design acknowledges a number of ways to enhance the built environment and benefits are explained by different communities of practice. Nevertheless, these are often limited views that overlook a level of detail we see in graphic objects and do not fall within the typical education of a built environment professional. An architect may have once studied architectural lettering, but that knowledge and understanding has not evolved sufficiently to cope with the communication complexity of contemporary city life. The design and selection of a typeface, design for a banner, or the ubiquitous nature of some basic human mark-making activity such as the standard white line on roads, pathway or sports field would not be considered as core concerns. These are images and objects, but how might such simple but effective devices be understood as contributing significantly to the image of the city? Having alluded to this from a historical perspective, for example, Johnston's lettering for London, this question will be further addressed in Chapter 4.

4

Imageability

'... that quality in a physical object which gives it a high probability of evoking a strong image in any given observer'.

LYNCH 1960: 9

Introduction

This chapter and Chapter 5 which follows, applies the arguments outlined in Chapter 1 to ideas and concepts prevalent in urban design, respectively about *image* and the *visual*. Chapter 4 analyses the way urban design has analogized city design by using the printed page as a metaphor, an approach also used by others. We explore problems associated with the word sign and implications regarding scale. The chapter will appropriate the macro–micro duality as a theoretical and empirical distinction to further the earlier mentioned mesodomain as a position that connects people to places through graphic representation.

Whereas Chapter 3 showed how inscription is both a spatial and temporal intervention, the two main case studies in this chapter illustrate how imageability is revealed through a concentration and plurality of eclectic graphic interventions in Shinjuku, Tokyo, and a more sparsely but systematically applied singular design in the City of Westminster, London.

The chapter asks the question: How do urban graphic objects contribute to the image of the city? It will focus specifically on Kevin Lynch's notion of the city image and its elements. By superimposing the idea of the urban graphic object introduced in the previous chapter onto Lynch's five elements of the city image (paths, edges, nodes, districts, landmarks), the intention is to explain how the modern city image is determined through graphic elements, and thus contribute to the physical qualities that enhance identity, structure and meaning associated with imageability.

A simple thought experiment illustrates the principle guiding this part of the book. Close your eyes and think of a zebra. What is it you see? What most resembles the zebra? Its shape? The black and white striped pattern? The most likely answer is patterned black and white stripes superimposed on an animal resembling a cross between a mule and horse. The mental image induced here is so vivid it may be referred to as graphic.

An urban-graphic analogy

Chapter 1 introduced the spatial dimension of graphic activity. This proposed how what were referred to as 'real spaces' become symbols because they are marked symbolically. Derived from a psychologist's perspective, this endorsed how micro psychology provides a basis for understanding the minor anxieties, pleasures, structures, events, and decisions that contribute to everyday life. But the alignment of real and printed spaces relied on the use of analogy. In this context, the printed page provided a useful visual analogy for scaling up an understanding of how to read the environment through a set of symbols to guide future actions as the so-called product of graphic engineering. Moles attempted to elevate the idea of graphic design to something more than simply applying an aesthetic sensibility to the design of a train timetable or yoghurt carton. He argued that our existence is increasingly symbolic in that, in certain circumstances, communication value is superior to material reality. We need only consider the values associated with police uniforms or the strip of our favourite football team, the importance of colour when buying a car, or the fluorescent orange traffic cone on the motorway, to grasp a basic understanding of this concept. Although situated within the environmental framework of everyday life, Moles's distinction of real space as objects, for instance a boulevard or street, is predominantly urban. These are the objects that substitute for printed matter. This ontological metaphor with emphasis on the visual field is an established analogy in urban design.

   Urban thinkers are accustomed to using analogy to better convey understandings of the city. For example, Lynch (1981: 82) uses the metaphor 'city as machine'. Through this approach, architecture and graphic communication have been directly linked by the suggestion that gothic cathedrals were '[t]he bibles and the encyclopaedias of both the illiterate and the literate' (Rowe and Koetter 1978: 48). Lynch (1960) pre-empted Moles by analogizing the intelligibility of the American cityscape using the same metaphor of the printed page. The legibility that Moles claimed is what Lynch alludes to when he writes 'Just as this printed page, if it is legible, can be visually grasped as a related pattern of recognizable symbols, so a legible city would be one whose districts or landmarks or pathways are easily identifiable and are easily grouped into an overall pattern' (Lynch 1960: 3). Moreover, the same allegory is used by Lefebvre (1996: 102) when comparing the city's 'objectality' to the 'cultural reality' of a written book.

   By contrasting the craft of page design with the complexity of city design the familiarity of the page acts as a synonym for the more challenging recognition and coherence of the cityscape. However, although Lynch used the analogy to convey the idea of legibility, he did not explore the nature of page design, which in his own book *The Image of the City*, utilized typographic and non-typographic elements, photographs, diagrams and drawings to enhance the text and assist the reader. Lynch features photographs of directional signs and other graphic devices appear in photographs of Journal Square in Jersey City, the Civic Centre and Broadway in Los Angeles, Boston's subway, Washington and Summer Streets, and Scollay Square. These devices are predominantly typographic, but a clock, flag, car registration plate and a picture of a motorcar also feature in photographs, as Lynch links signs and other details such as arrows to the legibility of the cityscape.

Legibility in the Lynch sense is determined by the recognition of parts and the coherence with which these form an overall pattern, maintaining that a good mental image of the environment contributes to the creation of a harmonious relationship between humans and their surroundings. For him, identity, meaning and structure characterize the environmental image formed, in part, by the physical quality of objects that make a place legible. Legibility in this sense is also referred to as '*imageability*', '*visibility*' or '*apparency*' in the city as an artistic object. His primary interest is the composite image of the city object, 'sharp' and 'intense', 'well-formed', 'distinct', and 'remarkable', derived from all the senses, socially and emotionally important (Lynch 1960: 10). Everyday objects such as lettering, house numbers, street names, traffic signs, directional signs, glaring signs and signs as wayfinding devices – all invariably mentioned by Lynch – are seen as part of this environmental image. The appearance of these match the aspirations of the composite image of the city object, consistent with the introduction of graphic objects in Chapter 1 where they were introduced as affective vivid visual devices.

This inconspicuous urban-graphic analogy is introduced in Lynch's seminal work, said to be the most read book on urban design (LeGates and Stout 2003: 424). Although Moles appears unaware of the earlier use of the same analogy, by comparison Lynch recognized the work of European and American psychologists on orientation but considered it 'sketchy', believing their approach to be too individualistic. Seeking a more generalized view, he prioritized the common mental pictures held by the majority of people. The analogy will, therefore, be familiar to many environmental professionals, if meaningless because Lynch is better known for the identification of five types of elements that contribute to the images of the city: paths, edges, districts, nodes, and landmarks.

The printed page analogy used by Lynch and Moles did not go beyond acknowledging a related pattern of recognizable symbols on a page. Yet, on a basic level typography, photography, and illustration (as elements of graphic design) provide basic clues for understanding the patterns and symbols that comprise page design, and thus may be transferred for environmental analysis. As Chapter 1 expanded the notion of graphic design by establishing a foundation for urban graphic objects and urban graphicacy, the question arises as to what extent the ideas associated with these concepts contribute to what Lynch (1960: 46–90) referred to as 'the city image and its elements'.

Having elevated the frequently used analogy of reading a book compared to reading the city, the next section contemplates how graphic elements impact on the elements that contribute to the city image, by up-scaling the typographic and graphic detail of page design to something more akin to city size.

The city image and its [graphic] elements

According to Lynch, an integrated network of paths, edges, districts, nodes, and landmarks make up the elements of the city image, and contribute to identity, structure and meaning. This provides a useful framework for thinking about graphic design as urban design, and graphic objects as urban objects, because it is an acknowledged approach in urban design. Although not an explicit part of Lynch's study, graphic elements are implicitly part of the urban fabric. As we have seen, these have proved difficult to categorize on an urban scale, even though they contribute significantly to the visual, aesthetic and cultural identity of the city.

Graphic elements pepper Lynch's explanation of the city image and its elements. A *path* – the main city element according to most people in his study – is a street, walkway, transit line, canal, or railroad, along which other elements are present. People move along them; consequently they are places from which to observe the city. Floor texture, colour, facades, lighting patterns, signs, arrows, house numbering as scaling devices, identifying check points, planting, naming and numbering. All enhance the visual scope of path design. An *edge* is a linear boundary and barrier (with varying degrees of permeability) or seam that unites or isolates areas, examples of which are given as shores, railroads, cuts, edges of development, or walls. Like paths, they too may be directional but differ in that they are not generally distinguished through the movement of people. Lynch provides no examples of graphic elements at edges, but a 'welcome' place name on a roadside is an obvious signifier of crossing a boundary, illustrating how paths and edges intersect as well as signalling the transition from one district to another. *Districts* are different in that they are medium-to-large sections of the city with an inside and outside, both experienced within and discernable outwith. 'Texture, space, form, detail, symbol, building type, use, activity, inhabitants, degree of maintenance, and topography' at various scales provide the physical characteristics of a district and Lynch provides the example of lettering on signs as a small-scale example of an object identified with a district (1960: 68). (The representation of path, edge and district are exemplified in the later case study on the City of Westminster street nameplate.) More strategic than districts are *nodes*, which exist at either a small or large scale depending on context. Much more intensive than a district, a node may be a junction, crossing, transition or break point, as simple as a street corner or enclosure of some kind. These may be small scale or as large as the city itself, depending on its relative position. A subway station entrance, major railway station, or an airport, exemplifies this category. Finally, different to a node for being a memorable object (although something may fit both categories), a *landmark* is an object that stands out from its background and is unique. Given examples would be: a gold dome; an object that has spatial prominence; something related to a particular activity such as worship; or as obscure as an isolated traffic light, street name, sign or store front, single traffic light or street name, innumerable signs, store fronts, trees, doorknobs, and other urban detail (Lynch 1960: 48). Each of these elements is open to interpretation by users and may be configured differently in the sense that 'an expressway may be a path for the driver, and edge for the pedestrian'. A central area may be a district when a city is organized on a medium scale, and a node when an entire metropolitan area is considered (1960: 48).

In sum, amongst Lynch's explanation of what constitutes an element, and how people recall five key components that make up the city image, countless visual interventions occur that are graphic interventions. Many of these are acknowledged and the relationship between urban and graphic is clear with respect to how these contribute to imageability. As noted earlier in Chapter 1, these applications are at best described as a miscellaneous range of things and far from anything that might be called a typology. Each are linked with different aspects of studying the city. For example, texture and colour feature in discussion about the fabric of towns, alongside scale, style, character, personality and uniqueness (Cullen 1971: 11), and the 'innumerable signs' mentioned by Lynch closely align with how the word sign is used in relation to lettering in the environment (Baines and Dixon 2003), illustrating a specific context for the word sign.

This use of the word *sign* is problematic as it emphasizes the gap between relatively small- and large-scale interventions. For example, the word sign is used by Lynch in different ways: it refers to a 'yellow-lettered sign' (1960: 180) as well as Boston's 'bright gold dome' as a 'key sign' (1960: 82). Moles is similarly abstract when referring to signs in non-materialistic ways as 'symbolic element shapes' such as 'arrows, shingles, posters, signals, and so forth' to 'represent things or actions' (1989: 120). His use, from a perspective of 'micropsychology' is scaled towards everyday 'micro-scenarios' and scrutiny of 'micro-anxieties, micro-pleasures, micro-structures, micro-events, or micro-decisions', something referred to as 'the entire web of life' (1989: 119). Lynch acknowledges relatively small and large objects, from lettering to domes, whereas Moles aligns ideas about graphic design, legibility and universality to the detail of everyday life. Scale is, therefore, an important dimension for understanding the urban fabric but the word sign is inadequate for understanding urban graphic objects in the physical sense, compared to the semiotic sense (discussed in more detail in Chapter 6). The next section introduces how the problem associated with scale has been dealt with by others, and formulates an approach to scale that bridges different interpretations of the word sign.

Problems associated with sign and scale

In interdisciplinary discourse about everyday objects that aspire to make the world more legible we have seen how *sign* is a word used to designate easily identifiable things such as a shop front. But it also indicates an architectural feature such as a dome! This is both problematic and useful for our purpose here. A sign is a signal, gesture, notice, symbol or word indicating the likely presence, occurrence or initiation of something else. In the broadest sense, a sign can be anything that conveys meaning and 'there is nothing that is not potentially or actually a sign' (Mitchell 1986: 62). The distinction between these uses of the word for understanding the potential range of urban graphic objects allows the possibility for a multitude of objects to be identified as graphic objects. The context is key here, but when the word is used within a single discipline to mean different things, as is the case with Lynch, it is confusing and therefore problematic. It's often unclear whether he means a traffic sign, such as an arrow indicating one-way street, or a landmark building. Whilst both are clearly signs, the difference between the two in terms of physical reality is obvious.

To overcome this confusion, the distinction between 'sign' and 'SIGN' has been employed to respectively differentiate between everyday use such as a sign on a shop front or a directional sign on a footpath, and how semioticians associate the word with anything that has meaning (Mollerup 2005: 11). The latter acknowledges how the word is used in the study of semiological schema in the relationship between signifier, signified and sign (Barthes [1957] 2009: 131–87). For example, a structure such as the Empire State Building in New York is a SIGN – perhaps that you are approaching Manhattan – but not a sign in the same sense as the inscription that labels it 'EMPIRE STATE'. This typographic differentiation helps us to migrate between two kinds of urban graphic object – typically those that name, direct, describe and regulate or those that serve a different primary purpose, such as provide shelter or accommodation.

SIGN in the semiotic sense helps us understand meaning. Categorized in this way, it enables us to consider the Empire State Building as a semiotic symbol, regardless of the professional design disciplines that contributed to the building's form. In the case of the Empire State Building, most often it will be associated with architecture, but here it is also considered an urban graphic object for particular reasons. For example, when the building's silhouette is seen as part of the Manhattan skyline and its shape alone is pre-eminent, its identity and meaning contribute to the 'vitality, power, decadence, mystery, congestion, greatness, or what you will' of that place (Lynch 1960: 8–9). Seen from afar, the Empire State Building is a vivid image, distinct from its surroundings. The same can be said for the decorative gold lettering that adorns its façade, embedded in the building's fabric. The letter shape and colour are designed to stand out, in the same way as the building's Art Deco appearance, height and shape. The familiar shape and gold inscription both stand out through their distinctive form. See Plate 5.

If valued for these visual qualities alone, the Empire State Building is an ancillary graphic object as well as a product of architecture. It provides a distinct graphic image of New York. The building's lettering is a primary graphic object because its form serves no other purpose than to identify the building, whereas the building itself serves different functions.

Signs are thus signs and SIGNS, and Mollerup depicts the relationship between the two as concentric circles suggesting some sort of scalar relationship, confirming that the narrow interpretation of sign is contained within the broader SIGN. Mollerup provides a basic distinction for comparing relatively small-scale objects such as architectural lettering or a road sign with the large-scale products of architecture and other built environment professionals.

In the case of the Empire State Building, our understanding of the object is based on more than either lettering or architecture, neither of which can be seen as one. For example, the building's silhouette, when seen from afar, may emphasize the pinnacle but its inscription is obviously concealed from view. Similarly, when looking up at the building from the ground level, the inscription is seen in full but its pinnacle is obscured. If framed as macro-micro perspectives, a fusion appears to take place at a meso level to emphasize a more comprehensive understanding of what the building means in the national psyche. For example, the United States flag is set against the building's façade as it continues to soar upward. At ground level, the inscription labels what the object is, and its status as an American cultural 'icon' is in part represented through the close association with the Stars and Stripes. The building's defining summit is invisible and the smallest of its defining properties, the detailed vertical ridges embedded in the gold of the building's inscription is similarly unacknowledged.

FIGURE 4.1 *View from street level of the Empire State Building in New York.*

Having briefly identified in this section some concerns associated with sign and scale, the macro–micro duality has been introduced as a possible remedy to explain how sign and scale can be used to amalgamate the two and overcome narrow and broad meanings associated with the word sign. How might this be used? The next section attempts to frame an approach.

Concerning mesographic analysis

The macro–micro duality is an established concept in disciplines such as sociology or economics. By comparison it is less understood and therefore underused in design, but there is some evidence for its use. In Art Nouveau, Barilli (1969: 36) uses it to describe William Morris' integration of macrostructure with microstructure when comparing Gaudi's concern for railings, balustrades, gratings, door handles, furnishings, furniture and windows. In graphic communication, Walker (1995: 87) describes the London Underground map as a microcosmic model that represents the macrocosmic system of the railway network. In typography, Twyman (1982: 2–22) describes both inter-character and inter-word spacing as micro level concerns against the macro-level activity of spacing larger units of text. Furthermore, in typography, Stöckl (2005: 204–14) uses the distinction whilst referring to microtypography, mesotypography, macrotypography and paratypography, showing how a scale of concerns adapt to larger and larger units of analysis. A common perception of the macro–micro issue is, therefore, that it refers to the very small or very large. Yet, in other fields such as Sociology, it is recognized as an analytical tool for its theoretical and empirical distinction, as a philosophical dualism, and to emphasize an 'agency–structure/individual–society' dualism'.

As an empirical distinction, large and small immediately present a way of understanding the macro–micro, whereas the theoretical perspective leads to abstract connotations deployed in social science and science scenarios in disciplines as diverse as geography or pharmacy. From a philosophical perspective, a distinct *here* or *there* scenario contrasts with a mutually integrated scenario where the macro and micro are interwoven. This is where the mesodomain or mesostructure take prominence. Again, borrowing from sociology, this acknowledges that interaction happens in a region where two contrasting scaled entities fuse into a unit of greater meaning (Marshall 1998: 410). In writing about the meso level, Ward (1902: 629–58) refers to mesography as 'knowledge of "human nature" derive[d] from the social environment'. By the same sentiment, the mesographic level stands for the way humans interact with their environment through graphic objects that are both physical and meaningful. Can we therefore construct a macro/meso/micrographic theory that spans the sign-SIGN duality and provides a model for analysing the synthesis of graphic objects between small, medium, large and extra large?

Macrographic and micrographic are established words, but only the latter warrants a mention in a short dictionary definition for *micrograph*: a photograph taken by a microscope. Micrographic is related to the word microgram; a photograph or drawing of an object under the microscope. It is closely associated to the seventeenth-century term micrography, traced to Robert Hooke's 1665 book *Micrographia* about physiological descriptions of minute objects (such as a flea, or fish scales) made possible by the use of magnifying glasses. Micrographic in this sense describes the technique of representation made possible by a particular technology enabling the observation of something previously considered invisible. A micrographic object is therefore imperceptible, except at close quarters.

A simple example illustrates how the macro–meso–micro continuum works. A life-size illustration of housefly has been placed in the men's urinals at Schiphol Airport. The impact is claimed to increase the attention, aim and accuracy of men urinating, thus reducing spillage by 80% (Thaler and Keller [2008] 2009: 4). See Figure 4.2.

Viewed from left to right, the urinal attracts men towards the place they should pee. As one moves closer, a fly in the urinal comes into view, synthesizing with the urinal and drain holes. At this point, form and context are at their most affective. We will call this the mesographic level. If the fly were isolated from the other objects, as seen in

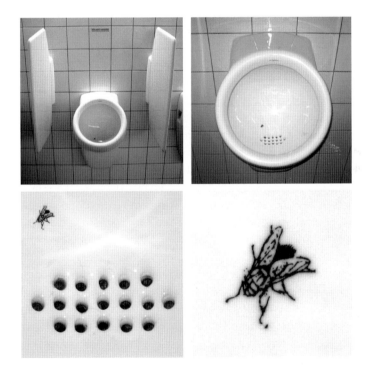

FIGURE 4.2 *Fly-in-urinal, Schiphol Airport, The Netherlands (Schiphol Airport, The Netherlands (2011)).*

This graphic intervention impacts on behaviour, and demonstrates how a synthesis of object-to-object relationships is most affective at the meso-level.

the final photograph of the sequence, it is meaningless by comparison. The fly is a sign within a SIGN, a micro object most affective at the meso level where it synthesizes with other objects, but indistinguishable at the macro level when the urinal is viewed from afar. It is isolated at the micro level when divorced from its context. At some point in the experience of taking a pee, the urinal, fly and drain communicate collectively and cohesively to influence behaviour.

Analysing this sequence reinforces the view that, in this instance, graphic intervention is most affective at the intermediate level shown in the middle two images, where the graphic image of a fly comes into view. If the statistics are to be believed, its impact is significant. This happens in the mesodomain where the image of the fly is connected to the image of the drain and the utility of the urinal as a whole. At the mesographic level cause and effect are interwoven in ways less visible and affective at the macrographic or micrographic level. This scenario, copied in other 'public' toilets such as Oslo airport (where a golf hole and flag replace the housefly) is humorous but effective. The principle may also be applied to other environmental contexts.

Figure 4.3 shows three environmental contexts – a pedestrian crossing, a round-about and a commemorative garden. Each displays graphic elements as part of the urban fabric. The pedestrian sign conveys destinations; the chevron suggests direction; the multitude of crosses emphasizes the number of war dead. Reading these images from left to right illustrates how a change in scale moves us between macro–meso– micrographic levels. Each stage may be analysed for the message's intention, but the mesographic level is where the intended communication happens: a black rectangle with clear typography synthesizes the functioning sign; a single chevron determines the direction of travel; a repetition of white Latin crosses, poppy flowers and names commemorate the number of war dead. In each context the micrographic detail of the apostrophe, the brick, the poppy, are overlooked. At the larger scale, the black rectangle, repeated chevron pattern and arrangement of white Latin crosses are understood as part of the environment but do not inform, instruct or incite to the same degree.

If the scale of analysis is adjusted, and the environmental context omitted, the same macro–meso–micro analysis can be applied to smaller objects. For example, the shape of the letter s may be examined as a macrographic object, at the mesographic level with its familiar open counters and diagonal spine, or the micrographic detail of the serif terminals at the end of the stroke, or the change in line thickness at the spine. Or, the white Latin cross (a micrographic component in an environmental context) also works at the macrographic level as a synthesis of the crucifix shape, typographic panel and poppy image, or the mesographic level when each aspect is considered independently, or the micrographic level as individual properties. For example, the name of the dead soldier is made up of individual letters that, when arranged, form a recognizable word.

This part of our discussion attempts to convey how the mesographic level is useful for assessing the role of the graphic object in the built environment, as an intermediate

FIGURE 4.3 *Three macro–meso–micrographic scenarios (London, UK (2009); Northampton, UK (2011); Market Harborough, United Kingdom (2010)).*

Reading from left to right, top to bottom, meaningful synthesis happens more at the mesogaphic level when individual properties unify to convey a primary message. The apostrophe, brick and poppy are details often overlooked, but when arranged to convey meaning at a larger scale or as part of a composite group, these may better satisfy environmental communication intentions.

stage between sign and SIGN. It also illustrates how graphic objects at this level most affect human behaviour.

Using this kind of analysis is highly relevant in wayfinding. For example, contemplate the sequence of images in Figure 4.4 depicting the experience of visiting the Olympic Stadium in Montreal. Travelling to the stadium to watch an event is facilitated by graphic representation on many levels. Survey the images left to right, top to bottom, referring to the photographic sequence from 1–9. The silhouette of the stadium in photograph 1 with its prominent viewing tower on the horizon identifies the venue and stands out in the city horizon. Much closer, photograph 2 depicts the approach to the stadium

FIGURE 4.4 *Visiting the Montreal Olympic Stadium (Montreal, Canada (2010)).*
The components that facilitate the visitor experience of attending an Olympic event are dependent on graphic intervention object-to-object and object-to-space relations on many levels.

dominated by the same object still defined by its distinctive shape, but now with more detail in view. On entering the building, the 1976 Montreal Olympic Games emblem is applied to the glass door, with the symbolism of the building exterior having disappeared at this point (see photograph 3). The scaling then repeats as the visitor enters the swimming arena and must find their seat. Beginning with photograph 4, seating is recognizable in red but too numerous to locate a specific seat without the assistance of signs featuring letters and numbers placed within a distinct blue rectangle, as seen in photograph 5. This acts as an orientation device that leads to individual seating, each containing a location number in black on a rectangular metal plate on the underside of each seat, as seen in photograph 6. The visitor then orientates their view towards the swimming pool as seen in photograph 7. Its properties are determined in part by the lane lines, blue water and numbers that identify where competitors will stand, as shown in photograph 8. Finally, the eyes come to rest on the preferred contestants diving platform shown in photograph 9, defined in detail and in a sequence of numbers.

This sequence of visual SIGNs does not exactly comply with what Cullen (1971: 9) called 'serial vision' – the contrast between existing and emerging views as one walks through a town – but there is a what he also referred to as a 'coherent drama' in the way these variously scaled objects enhance an occasion.

In scalar terms, the building silhouette, seating pattern and swimming pool are macrographic objects that identify fixed places, whereas the experience of participation relies on mesographic relations between sign and SIGN that orientate us to a fixed position, then supported by micrographic details in the form of the games emblem, personalized seat number and the identification of a preferred competitor.

These examples attempt to show how Moles' concern for the micro-scenarios balances with the macro-scenarios and, by default, include meso-scenarios whereby a synthesis of graphic form happens. It provides a framework for evolving Lynch's penchant for imageability and the micrographic form of lettering or house numbers to the macrographic form of the city skyline. In between, a mesographic fusion serves to unify objects in meaningful ways that affect behaviour. What happens as people move between the micro-meso-macro domains will not be explained here – that is the work of more scientific fields such as cognitive psychology and their concern for how the mind connects with the world. Those wishing to investigate further will discover more about such matters as visual perception, the abstract concept of information, representational content, and visual objects. When referring to visual objects, cognitive psychologists speak of how visual elements function in reasoning through 'defining properties' and 'configurational pattern', central to their concern for 'the connection between mind and world' and 'how vision is able to select or pick out or refer to individual things in a scene' (Pylyshyn 2007: 1–30). Lynch's interpretation of legibility, and graphic intervention, simultaneously seek to enable this.

Our interest here is in defining the properties, patterns and purpose of urban graphic objects. A need to do this is, in part, because of an uncertainty about what constitutes graphic elements in cities. What are the defining properties and configurational patterns associated with urban graphic objects? To explore this in more detail we return to Lynch's city elements and attempt to define the graphic image at the *district* level in Shinjuku, Tokyo, the largest of megacities.

Shinjuku Ward, Tokyo

Chaotic, complex, and contradictory. These are some of the adjectives that characterize Tokyo, and Shinjuku displays all of these in abundance. As one of Tokyo's 23 city wards, its defining landmarks include the skyscraper district to the west that includes the monumental Tokyo Metropolitan Government Building (or City Hall) and the red light and entertainment district of Kabukichō to the northeast, incorporating the bohemian Golden Gai. Shinjuku emerged as one of five megacentres in the 1968 Tokyo City Plan. At its core is the large entertainment, business and shopping area above Shinjuku

Station, the junction of several suburban railway lines said to be the world's busiest railway station with approximately 3 million people passing through each day.

The ward typifies the development of Tokyo in the second half of the twentieth century, much of which was driven by railway companies who created sub-centres around their stations. Today there are few buildings in Tokyo more than 40 years old due to the Second World War, which reduced it to ruins. The destruction, much of it due to firebombing, resulted in people establishing urban villages of temporary accommodation resembling shanties, some of which still remain in stark contrast to the megastructural forms that emerged during Tokyo's reconstruction.

Shinjuku is a meganode in a megalopolis, a place often at the top of things to do in Tokyo due to its scale and variety. At one extreme, the City Hall provides panoramic views of the city that contrast with the intimacy of Golden Gai, promoted to tourists as a literary and artistic place to hang out. However, the sheer quantity, variety and irregularity of graphic objects in Shinjuku means the formal analysis of these things is challenging. We, therefore, turn to Lynch's city elements of paths, edges, nodes, and landmarks to establish how graphic objects are distributed in Shinjuku.

Through the variety of identification, information and instruction sign systems that facilitate Tokyo's rail transport infrastructure, Shinjuku's spatial importance as a networked place is apparent in the messages that assist passengers on their journeys. These signs lead in and out of the rail network to convey a hierarchy of information designed to influence passenger behaviour. However, the repetition, continuity and variation of graphic devices that identify a myriad of passenger choices reinforce Tokyo's identity rather than listing Shinjuku as more prominent than other destinations in the city's network. Not until Shinjuku's regional landmarks are signed to assist disembarkation, such as the Tokyo Metropolitan Government Office, does place identity start to take prominence.

The skyscraper district is not only dominated by the City Hall complex but also a host of other buildings with facades patterned with horizontal and vertical grid lines that characterize much of Tokyo's modern buildings. The exception amongst Shinjuku's skyscrapers is the Mode Gakuen Cocoon Tower – an elliptical building wrapped in arbitrary cross-linked diagonal lines resembling the concept of a cocoon. Its shape and irregular line-covered exterior distinguish it, typifying the definition of a landmark and point-reference that stands out.

In the immediate vicinity of the City Hall a double-layered road system dissects the central plaza and twin towers, epitomizing the road and sidewalk system in much of Tokyo's new development. In contrast to the Kabukichō district or Shinjuku Station, within relatively vast spaces graphic objects are sparse; buildings and transport routes dominate. Sidewalks are embedded with a yellow tactile paving strip for the visually impaired, contrasting with the neutral colour of the sidewalk, and other objects such as promotional banners, parking signs and navigation maps are carefully placed to complement the surroundings. Compared to two decade ago, facades display dual language names, as do other signs, whilst sculptural objects by internationally acclaimed artists such as Roy Lichtenstein or Robert Indiana provide smaller landmarks such as those at the i-LAND complex. Patterned floorscapes, uniformed workers, and illuminated 'walk' signs are a selective assortment of graphic objects on display. See Plate 6.

We mostly see examples at ground level that are accessible to the general public. However, a view from higher up indicates how elevated surfaces and structures are also space for a spectacle in a city as big as Tokyo. Masts, helipads, advertising structures, even running tracks and swimming pools, all stand out for their graphic form from an otherwise subdued cityscape. These objects, no less important in their intention than traffic signs or public art, function in the city's stratosphere.

Exiting Shinjuku Station in the direction of the Skyscraper District is a gradual transition through an enclosed pedestrian pathway very much like moving between terminals in an airport, with directional signage interspersed with commercial graphic nodes. For example, recessed from the main thoroughfare is the entrance to a McDonald's branch, suddenly appearing as a rich texture of light, colour, photography, lettering, freestanding and sculptural promotional objects designed to provide quick information about the products within.

Exiting Shinjuku Station in the direction of Kabukichō (from the East exit) is quite different to the Skyscraper District. An explosion of graphic objects is more sudden, and the traveller is directly confronted with the towering façade and popular meeting place of Studio Alta. This provides a taste of the visual spectacle that defines much of the area, and is at its most intense two blocks further north at Yasakuni Dōri, the edge of Kabukichō. The entrance to Kabukichō is signalled by a 'torii' (gate); beyond this is a dense display of signs along Kabukichō Ichibangai, each side of the street covered with protruding signs that obliquely obliterate any sense of original building façades up to Bunka Sentā-dōri. At night the signs illuminate to dominate the street scene. Eating places, arcades, batting centres, host bars, peep shows, cabaret, love hotels and fetish bars provide the entertainment, attraction and visual stimulation, and further in to the east, the small alleys and two storey buildings of the Golden Gai contrast with the openness and comparatively sterile nature of the Skyscraper District. The intimate streets, wide enough only for pedestrians or cyclists, are laden with Japanese and English signs featuring well-known beers and spirits.

Amidst the visual clutter determined by the excessive display of graphic objects, the inner part of Kabukichō offers little of architectural distinction, compared to the monumental Tokyo Metropolitan Government Building or the metaphorical quirkiness of the Mode Gakuen Cocoon Tower. The exceptions are Minoru Takeyama's post-modern *Niban-kan* building and the more sedate *Hanazono-jinja* temple. Both landmarks make distinct architectural statements but with different intentions, standing out for their reliance on bold use of colour. For example, the visual appearance of *Hanazono-jinja* relies heavily on its bright red exterior, as dominant as the mass of colour the international high street retailers use to reinforce their brand identity. See Plate 7.

Colour, in this sense, plays a dominant role in the legibility of these landmarks, and is relied on to both emphasize and reinforce other key messages in the Shinjuku Ward. It singles out stand-alone sections and fixed objects, enhancing important parts of Shinjuku's infrastructure such as the railway underpass, pedestrian and vehicle signs, destinations, public art and performance objects. Bold primary and secondary colours, often applied flat is a common occurrence and the subtle modelling of colour, shape, form and scale in a billboard illustration has no less impact or visibility. They are all designed to alert the senses. See Plate 8.

This glimpse of the Shinjuku Ward, comparing the contrasting areas of the Skyscraper District to the west and the Kabukichō area in the northeast provides a partial visual perspective on the variety of graphic objects that persist in the urban fabric. The Shinjuku Station node is on the north–south axis of a transit line, permeable at points where graphic design is apparent and most intense. The pedestrian signs within the station, and the point at which Yasakuni Dōri meets the railway line and cars pass underneath the tracks, exemplify this (also see Plate 8).

Shinjuku is a meganode in a megalopolis, but the intensive foci that distinguishes the entrance to Kabukicho Ichibangai through one of its defining visual features – the torri structure – flashing and functioning as a defining night-time landmark in the district, is a node within a meganode. This is in stark contrast to the multi-layered urban structure of walkways and roads that cross at the base of the landmark City Hall complex. There, the variety of entertainment choice is much less an environmental concern, except for the restaurants and public art placed at strategic points as limited examples for leisure and pleasure.

The examples provide a sense of variety but there is nothing that visually links one area to the other, except the consistent use of writing systems as a representation of language predominantly in Japanese and sometimes English. This is the main unifying graphic element. Other than our own sense of place and spatial awareness, neither the Skyscraper District nor Kabukichō display any visual identification with the Shinjuku Ward beyond the presence of its name on signs at Shinjuku Station. Compared to European cities such as London or Paris, local identity at the district level is ever present, as we will next explore. Having defined how graphic objects contribute to two contrasting pedestrian experiences of Shinjuku, characterizing very different local place identities, this is next considered from a single object perspective using the City of Westminster street nameplate in London.

City of Westminster street nameplate, London

Surrounding the City of London, 32 boroughs collectively make up Greater London. One of these is the City of Westminster, the only other borough to have city status. Established in 1965 after the London Borough Act 1963, it encompasses the districts of Covent Garden, Soho, Pimlico, Belgravia, Knightsbridge, Marylebone, St Johns Wood, Maida

Vale, Mayfair, Bayswater, St James's, Victoria, Paddington and Queens Park. Bordered by the City of London, the boroughs of Camden and Brent, and Kensington & Chelsea, the City of Westminster meets the River Thames to the south. Its central location includes the notable landmarks of Buckingham Palace, the Houses of Parliament, Downing Street, and parts of London's West End such as Oxford Street, Piccadilly and Soho, making it a place of great architectural and historical importance. With 1,753 streets covering 200 miles, and 400 miles of footways there are said to be 63,000 items of street furniture. Across the district the City of Westminster street nameplate is omnipresent and is one of the most common elements of physical infrastructure that identifies the borough.

Considered by the borough as an 'iconic' object in the public realm, it was designed by Chris Timings at Design Research Unit in 1967 and its form has endured since then. From fashion to fridge magnets, the sign design has been appropriated beyond utility to function as an aspirational object. See Plate 9. The basic design is comprised of a landscape white rectangle (with round corners when not framed), aligned left black typography for the street name and abbreviated postcode highlighted in red, and a fine rule running across the width of the nameplate above the borough name. The nameplate is often fixed to a vertical surface such as a wall or railings, and two posts support a freestanding version are also in use. There does not appear to be a single-pole mounted option.

These basic graphic elements provide a reliable recognizable image varying only in size and street name (there are roads, terraces, mews, and gates as well). A restrained arrangement displays the location name and postcode in one size and the borough name in smaller capitals across the bottom in a typeface resembling the sans-serif typeface Univers Bold Condensed. Street names as short as Bow Street or as long as Buckingham Palace Road fit on one or two lines.

The sign arrangement exhibits pioneering design characteristics developed in the early twentieth century, resembling the early experimental typographic design work of El Lissitzky, who was strongly influenced by the Suprematist artist Kasimir Malevich. Lissitzky introduced typographic elements into his painting and used black and red to the same effect as much of the early modern typography. For instance, the rule across the full width of the panel is reminiscent of the way Jan Tschichold used a line in his 1937 exhibition poster 'konstruktivisten'.

The layout conforms with ideas about clarity that emerged from Germany in the 1920s, and matured in Switzerland in the 1950s. It echoes the principles of what would become Swiss Design, or the International Typographic Style, set out by Jan Tschichold, an approach that broke with the tradition of symmetrical typography (e.g. ornamental typefaces, axial arrangement, inflexibility) and advocated, economy, precision, clarity, purity, standardization, and objectivity, based on the modernist mantra of Louis Sullivan's *form follows function*. Sans-serif typography, usually ranged left, epitomized progressive values for designers who used structure and harmony to communicate legible information. The nameplate design combined the early twentieth-century pioneering aspirations of modernist typography with the restraint and purity of Swiss

Design pioneers such as Joseph Müller-Brockmann. Asymmetric layout, rules to define parts of the picture plane and use of red contrasting with bold black sans-serif typography were the qualities that defined this approach.

The City of Westminster street nameplate has at its core a mid-twentieth century aspiration for legibility born out of early modernism. How does this relate to earlier notions of imageability and the elements of the city image? A focus on one London road provides some answers to this question.

According to London road signs, Exhibition Road – which runs in-between the Victoria and Albert Museum, and Natural History Museum – crosses the boundary of two boroughs; the City of Westminster to the north and the Royal Borough of Kensington and Chelsea to the south. Each end of the road displays an old and new sign, duplicating the road name. At a point closer to the middle of the road's length the two borough's sign variations are positioned in close proximity, providing a clue about where the borough border might be. These signs help people to locate themselves at district level. Contrasting nameplate designs that unify the respective areas differentiate the two boroughs.

Compared to the City of Westminster street nameplate, the nameplate in the neighbouring Royal Borough of Kensington and Chelsea stands in direct contrast and conforms with what Tschichold called 'old typography' ([1928] 1998: 66). This incorporates more decorative typeface designs, conforms to a symmetrical layout and includes punctuation (something superfluous in the Westminster design). The colour combination displays the location name in black and the borough name and postcode in red, and all signs have a thin black surround. The typography utilizes David Kindersley's *MoT Serif* typeface, created in 1952 for the British Ministry of Transport (and used in a number of UK towns and cities including Cambridge, Milton Keynes, Loughborough, Corby, and Runcorn) and the borough name appears in what resembles a decorative condensed blackletter style. Compared to the relative simplicity of the City of Westminster street nameplate, there are as many as four type sizes, the postcode is positioned awkwardly and often the asymmetrical convention, and additional arrows occasionally act as additional graphic devices. Overall, the various design elements collectively represent the antithesis of modernist aspirations evident in the Westminster design.

A testimony to City of Westminster street nameplate design's appeal is in the way it has been adapted and adopted to meet cultural and commercial appeal. For example, in London's Chinatown, the nameplate accommodates additional Chinese characters, or another variation promotes 'Theatreland' in locations such as Charing Cross Road and Haymarket. These retain the white rectangle, black and red colour scheme and typographic styling within a familiar format true to the original.

Such is the appeal of the City of Westminster street nameplate that more than 100 companies have exploited the design by copying its basic layout, often without consent. Consequently, in 2007, Westminster Council bought the nameplate copyright for £50,000 with a view to charging a licence fee to ensure that the design is protected when necessary. Variations on the basic design have since served the needs of television companies, estate agents, bars, merchandising, theatre production, also adapting for room signage, fashion and even fridge magnets (sold at the London Transport Museum for £2.99). Another London borough makes use of the same format. On Manchester United merchandising, the team crest is added to complement the place name, with the ground name of Old Trafford and its postcode highlighted in red. In contrast, a simpler version – used to sell a small housing development called Abbey Mews – utilizes the same sans-serif lettering in black and red, enough to evoke the aspiration of the original. Inauthenticity is easily detected in the London Borough of Newham's plagiarized version, whereby the location name is split by an exaggerated space that distances 'Westfield' from 'Avenue'; the postcode ranges to the right. Even when the typeface is changed to a serif font, as in the case of Louisa's Place in the town of Market Harborough, the similarity persists.

The enduring appeal of the nameplate partly reflects Westminster City Council's commitment to a code that directs all interventions in the city's public realm. The code guides the selection, design and placement of street furniture and surfacing materials following ten simple rules themed under the headings: quality; durability/sustainability; character; clutter free; continuity; containment; context; co-ordination; consistency; and cherish. These rules determine high-quality components, materials, scheme design, implementation, detailing and maintenance and support an ongoing quality agenda.

The nameplate is proclaimed as one of the best post-war British signs but the reason for its 'iconic' status – as referred to in the borough's literature – is unclear. One reason may be that it is an exemplar of modern design in the sense that its visual qualities can be traced to the historical core of modern art and design in the early twentieth century. The values associated with that period endure through a design still in use a half-century after it was first installed. Today, the basic design also perpetrates everyday life, imitated and valued for its visual clarity and as an object of visual culture, for its aspirational presence and commercial appeal, so much so that the original design has legal status. Other reasons for its status go beyond the sign itself. For example, installations are predominantly surface mounted with concealed fixings, thus limiting street clutter yet standing out from the borough's preference for black street furniture. Consistently applied, it enhances continuity, is geographically distinct, and much copied. However, the nameplate is also a paradox. Its implementation in the late 1960s rendered much of what it replaced redundant, some older street signs being as clear, some less so.

The systemic nature of the City of Westminster street nameplate illustrates what graphic design does best: it connects and relates people, subjects, objects and ideas with places and spaces. This is traced back from a contemporary object of visual culture in the form of a fridge magnet to an item of street furniture at the scale of a city borough, and further back to the origins of European modernism. At its inception in the 1960s, a visual arrangement based on principles established 50 years earlier continues to be appropriated 50 years later. This implies a durability of basic design principles that resist needless change, placing a high value on identity, structure and meaning on a spatial scale perhaps not previously seen in the signing of roads in a defined area. More fundamental is the reuse of defining properties in graphic design, such as the use of the centuries-old alphabet, an exemplar object of recycling, reuse and appropriation. Through synthesizing culture and commerce, the City of Westminster street nameplate has assumed new meanings in different contexts without undermining the integrity of earlier pioneering designers who were attracted by the relationship between art and society through design.

Summary

This chapter began by asking you to visualize a zebra in your 'minds eye'. It suggested that what came to mind were distinctive black and white stripes, these being more effective than a shape resembling something between a mule and horse. It is suggested that this is due to the graphic nature of the image; its vivid stripes. They stand out, even though they are perhaps more associated with 'the grand design' (Hawking and Mlodinow: 2010) than graphic design. Throughout the chapter we have tried to establish how such distinctiveness impacts on a city's image and its elements, by superimposing the notion of graphic objects explored in earlier chapters onto Lynch's ideas about imageability, legibility, and visibility. Lynch advocated vividness as an important quality in determining mental images of the environment, and this contributed to a classification of five elements that make up a city's image: paths, edges, nodes, districts and landmarks. The basis for the superimposition in this chapter is the fact that graphic communication in the form of the book has already provided a useful analogy for understanding the legible city. This extended discussion in Chapter 3, which aligned the development of writing systems with urbanization since early antiquity. Graphic design and urban design in this sense have been shown to be mutually enhancing, and both as contributors to the image of the city.

However, one of the key problems pointed out in this chapter is the lack of mutual understanding in language use. The distinction between sign and SIGN has been explained to overcome what others have respectively had to define as signboard or sign. Whereas the former jut out from walls, the latter may be what Calvino ([1972] 1997: 13–14) acknowledges as 'a print in the sand indicat[ing] a tiger's passage; a marsh announces a vein of water; the hibiscus flower, the end of winter'. To the 'sign' sensitive such ambiguity is a distraction, further exasperated by the relationship between sign and scale. The Empire State Building is a sign but not a signboard, and it was also used to explain the difference between sign and SIGN to introduce the semiotic perspective, which is explored further in Chapter 6. In an attempt to define an intermediate space between these two contrasting uses of the same word (Mollerup's convenience of capitalization is not enough), a new perspective on this has been introduced by borrowing from disciplines familiar with the use of macro-micro analysis to establish the notion of the mesographic object. This is where different objects synthesize into a higher unit of meaning than is available in less visible macro-micro states. Examples have been used to illustrate this concept, to emphasise when an arrangements of objects work together as defining properties to form a configurational pattern.

This chapter has shown how a single graphic object, if consistently applied can spatialize and unify a city district. The City of Westminster street nameplate identifies the borough through an object absent from the streetscape in Shinjuku. In keeping with the everyday nature of such an object, this has explained how procedures of delimitation mark boundaries through the organization of space, exemplifying how urban graphic objects regulate and illuminate changes in space. Moreover, a broader understanding of space locates the City of Westminster street nameplate as a spatial practice, satisfying Lefebvre's idea of spatial practice as outlined earlier in Chapter 2. The nameplate is an object of production and reproduction, seemingly promoting continuity and cohesion, competence and performance. No single object in that city, designed by built environment professionals, for example, Buckingham Palace, Oxford Street, Leicester Square, Hyde Park, defines the image of the City of Westminster in its entirety. Nor does the City of Westminster street nameplate. However, the nameplate does provide a unifying label more than any other urban object in that part of London. It serves as a constant element in the cityscape, and is operational on paths, at edges, as a node and landmark, as well as defining the district.

An apposite focus on Lynch's ideas about city image and its elements has been appropriate in this chapter because of his concern for legibility, and his use of the urban-graphic analogy. Although Lynch's ideas have since been criticized, and Lynch himself later questioned the prominence first given to legibility (Carmona *et al.* 2010: 113–17), his use of metaphor has been too inviting to overlook for augmenting a graphic design stance on the urban environment. Legibility is an established principle and well understood in type, typographic and graphic design, as well as in urban design. As a general concept it is defined as handwriting or print, clear enough to read, the latter originating from the Latin *legere*: to read. A key difference in the use of the term across two disciplines is the scale of application in the sense that the legible object might either be a letterform or a city. Legibility is a meaningful term that scales up or down. This is highly relevant to the arguments presented here because of a shared acceptance in usage. Built environment professionals associate it with Lynch's ideas about how the visual form of a city is ordered and intelligible. Graphic design professionals associate it with type and typographic design, and something that is clear to read such as the lettering on a motorway sign or the well-organized page of a book.

Although Lynch's ideas emerged more than 50 years ago, they are yet to fully impact on graphic design beyond the ideas associated with wayfinding and wayshowing. With this in mind, the next chapter will explore how urban objects fit within a more contemporary urban design framework that emphasizes the visual dimension of urban design and how this contributes to Alexander's notion of pattern language. Having emerged in the late 1970s, Alexander's work dealt with the scale at which urban design operates, through a series of patterns which although presented separately, are best understood in relation to each other. This encouraged us to think about places holistically in the pursuit of greater understanding. Graphic design is yet to be considered seriously as part of that appreciation, even though the product of its integrative practice lends itself well to understanding cities through the use of analogy by a number of theorists from urban design, psychology, and philosophy.

5

Pattern

'If the ensemble is a truckdriver plus a traffic sign, the graphic design of the sign must fit the demands made on it by the driver's eye'.

ALEXANDER 1964: 16

Introduction

Ideas about the city image and its elements have been influential in urban design. However, they have become more associated with the perceptual dimension of urban design (Carmona *et al.* 2010: 112–17). This chapter is concerned with the visual dimension of urban design. We explore the visual–aesthetic aspect of graphic design as urban design by focusing on the relationship between form and context within what Alexander (1964) called an ensemble, and how this form may be understood in what was later referred to as pattern language (Alexander *et al.* 1977). Building on examples introduced in Chapter 4, two models explain how the form and context relationship work in relation to Lynch's concern for identity meaning and structure. Further examples illustrate how new ensembles emerge, or fail to do so, as environmental changes in context are imposed by local pressures or natural forces. Two case studies extend the two pattern languages, namely the *Road Crossing* and *Ornamentation*, providing the opportunity to explain the wider context for everyday urban graphic objects. We will look at the highly visible 'zebra' crossing, and the more joyous visual qualities associated with the floorscape of Lisbon and São Paulo, leading us to associate visual–aesthetic concerns with visual culture. Moreover, this chapter responds to concerns that books on urban design overlook 'words, pictures and graphics' in the panoramas they portray; Alexander has been singled out in this regard (Scollon and Wong Scollon 2003: 144–45)

Identifying graphic objects as urban objects, tracing their existence through history, and exploring how these might fit within the image of the city has been our concern so far, the intention being to bring more specificity to the way urban thinkers have characterized what have been called 'miscellaneous urban objects'. At this point, we attempt to align graphic objects more closely with design so that the notion of graphic design within urban design can be more of a force in what urban design aspires to be: a process for making better places.

By establishing the notion of the *urban graphic object*, this differentiates graphic objects within the *urban object* that may stand for any urban element. Thus, graphic objects reside within urban objects, and graphic design may enhance urban design in a clear scalar relationship that locates the former within the latter. Exemplars of this concept have been discussed earlier, such as the carved inscription on a monument, a chevron on a roundabout, an event emblem on the door-to-sport venue, the façade pattern that wraps around a skyscraper or a street nameplate. Defining features in these are as much products of graphic design as any other discipline that aspires to contribute to the visual dimension of urban design.

In our earlier discussion about the dimensions of urban design – morphological, perceptual, social, visual, functional – at the end of Chapter 3, with the exception of morphology, it has shown that urban graphic objects significantly define most dimensions and design contexts of urban design. Graphic design, in whatever form it exists, is completely embedded in the design of urban environments at many levels, yet still it is largely unnoticed and insufficient time and interest has been committed to understanding its presence. Previous chapters have clearly evidenced this. As the scope for urban design is so wide, and graphic design is predominantly an art and design subject (at least in name), this chapter concentrates on the visual dimension of urban design to bring a tighter focus and deeper exploration of graphic design as urban design.

The visual dimension

The visual dimension of urban design is comprised of spatial and visual qualities, as well as artefacts. In this sense, spatial qualities differ from the way society and space is perceived in the social dimension, which is more aligned to the definitions cited from geography in Chapter 1. Our concern now is with the nature of artefacts, or visual elements in space that contribute to the visual dimension of urban design, and which of these exhibit some form of graphic address. This encompasses some of the defining features of the visual dimension of urban design such as monuments, façades, floorscape, street furniture and landscaping (Carmona *et al.* 2010: 184–200). At a basic level, these are self-explanatory in terms of how they incorporate graphic elements. A monument will usually display at the very least some lettering, sometimes combined with sculptural elements (think of the Arc de Triomphe). Façades may incorporate tactile and decorative material of the sort seen on a Gaudí building in Barcelona; floorscapes may also be distinct, such as the black and white patterned cobbled surfaces that define many Mediterranean public places; street furniture encompasses much diversity from direction signs or bollards or public art; and landscaping encapsulates hard and soft approaches that may comprise of differentiated textured surfaces for cars, cycles and pedestrians, to colourful flower arrangements. Collectively, these are inadequately portrayed by Carmona *et al.* (2010: 196–97) for cataloguing the full extent of graphic objects that adorn the townscape. Street furniture, in particular, is the most inappropriately titled because of the diversity it represents (e.g. the scope of public art within street furniture includes both sculpture and graffiti). The abundance of signage typically associated with Eastern cities is compared to the more modest approaches of European cities. Bollards are featured as a demonstration of how to separate cars from pedestrians. All these provide a highly selective assortment that bears only partial resemblance to the scope of objects identified so far in this book.

Identifying the visual elements of space in urban design from the perspective of graphic design is a more complex challenge if the visual–aesthetic dimension of urban design is to be fully understood from this perspective. Permanent and semi-permanent objects such as the markings on a sports pitch in a park, a textured floor surface for partially sighted people, illuminated decorations, topiary, a red carpet to celebrate a special occasion, warning tape masking an obstacle, or uniformed workmen on the street are all part of the city's visual aesthetic. See Plate 10.

Hence, as should be clear by now, the variety of things that constitute urban graphic objects is significantly more extensive than that portrayed in the urban design literature. Consequently, a collective understanding of graphic objects in urban objects is highly fragmented. We have already discussed in Chapter 1 that attempts to identify the nature of graphic design are either too narrow or all encompassing, are based on personal interpretations, or come from what graphic designers say they do. These are based more on professional practice rather than the expanded interpretation proffered in this book. The implication here is that when Carmona *et al.* (2010: 170) stress the importance of 'patterns and aesthetic order', because graphic objects have largely been overlooked in the communication function of cities, as noted earlier, their portrayal has been limited and consequently misunderstood. In order to simplify this, and work towards a more comprehensive theoretical understanding of the graphic form and urban context relationship, graphic interventions can be explained using well-established principles for urban design, as follows.

Form and context

Throughout this book we have tried to contextualize graphic objects beyond how they are portrayed in graphic design history and in the urban design literature. For example, the Trajan's Column inscription is a small, but central, part of Trajan's Forum. Consequently, the relationship between the two is underplayed. We have also seen how graphic objects dominate urban contexts to the point of visual and mental saturation, as in Tokyo's Kabukichō area. This contrasts with the more sedate and selective City of Westminster street nameplate, which delivers a regular prompt for the district's identity. These provided another interpretation of Lefebvre's representations of space and representational space, as noted in Chapter 2. The orderly City of Westminster street nameplate is a representation of space, whereas the graphic images in Kabukichō defines a representational space that embodies a gamut of complex symbolisms.

These contrasting examples of graphic objects in their urban context can be simplified into what Alexander (1964: 16) defined as an 'ensemble comprising the form and its context'. Although form and context are relatively straightforward terms, their importance for graphic design is reiterated by Davis (2012: 57): '[f]orm is that which we can shape, and context is the complement of factors that determines the nature of appropriate form'. This builds on Alexander's view that the fundamental purpose of design is form, whereby form means pattern or system. We have used 'object' to represent something visible or tangible, but this may also be interpreted in Alexander's use of form to mean 'pattern', something we will elaborate on below. What Alexander means by 'ensemble' takes us back to the visual dimension of urban design. An ensemble, according to Alexander, is explained as a suit and tie, the appropriateness of a certain move in chess, a musical composition, a truck driver and a sign whereby the 'graphic design' (meaning the sign) needs to fit with the driver's ability to see (Alexander (1964: 16). In all of these scenarios, appropriateness between form and context is determined by goodness of fit, meaning the suitability or rightness of the form and context relationship.

The issue of whether a tie matches a suit comes down to a sense of goodness of fit. Good fit happens as changing and multiple contexts make demands on form by defining and redefining the problems form must address. 'Design problems are *situated*, . . . solutions must respond to specific human motives and activities, conditions, and settings that may be viewed at a variety of scales or perspectives and across time' (Davis 2012: 57). In other words, changing context impacts on form, determining the congruity of fitness between two entities. Good fit happens when the demands of context – whatever they may be – are met by form, and there are numerous boundaries where form and context must unify for good fit to happen. In sum, Alexander (1964: 16) confirms:

> The form is part of the world over which we have control, and which we decide to shape while leaving the rest of the world as it is. The context is that part of the world which puts demands on this form; anything in that world that makes demands of the form is context. Fitness is a relation of mutual acceptability between these two. In a problem of design we want to satisfy the mutual demands which the two make on one another. We want to put the context and the form into effortless contact or frictionless coexistence.

Applying this theory to earlier examples, two distinct ensembles emerge that depict different relationships between form and context, affecting the identity, meaning and structure of the city image. The City of Westminster street nameplate fits its context on a number of levels by serving old and new demands. Most intentionally it names the road, but it also represents the permeability with neighbouring boroughs, as well as adapting to changes in local culture (as is the case with Chinatown and Theatreland). It unifies the area spatially, signals a key moment of change in direction, and stands out. All of this is achieved as a relatively small-scale object dispersed throughout the borough (district) at regular intervals, usually at the end of each street but sometimes along the street as well. Furthermore, its identification with London as a major capital city provides cultural connotations and commercial appeal that adapt to different economic demands beyond the geographic boundary of the district, as a representation of space and place. Its consistent application determines that in reinforcing the district identity no one part of the City of Westminster is prioritized over another. The more commercial Oxford Street is the same as the more residential Park Lane.

Alternatively, the abundance of illuminated signs in Kabukichō indicates that it is the entertainment district in Shinjuku. To walk along Kabukichō Ichibangai, day or night, exposes a sequence of signs that collectively impose themselves as a distinctive district image, illuminating by day the diversity of visual form, and illuminated at night as a dominating visual aesthetic. The Tokyo Convention and Visitors Bureau refer to Kabukichō Ichibangai as 'Electric Street'. On the approach from Shinjuku Station, the 'torri' defines the edge of this red light and entertainment district, as a node and landmark, and the array of signs define the primary activity of the street. There is no visual association with the wider Shinjuku Ward as the diversity of graphic form melds into one of the defining spatial features in the district, alongside Koreantown to the north and the Metropolitan Government Building complex to the west of Shinjuku Station. In Kabukichō, graphic forms amuse, attract and affect audiences in ways fit for purpose in an entertainment ensemble. They embody an all-encompassing layer of visual stimulation to the point that no other urban object – such as buildings – are able to compete for attention. More than defining a path, edge or node, these forms of graphic address, or 'discourses in place' (Scollon and Wong Scollon 2003), demarcate a wide footprint and, to some extent, is the district in that the perceptual dimension assumes greater prominence over the visual dimension. A sense of place is determined by the extent of collective graphic forms and their differing contextual demands, even subsuming the urban context. Both of these examples can be explained in models shown in Figure 5.1. These illustrate how the form and context relationship work for the selective implementation of the City of Westminster street nameplate and the more arbitrary application of illuminated signs in Kabukichō.

That being said, visual-aesthetic considerations do not always call for 'good fit' in the sense of a harmonious visual relationship with their surroundings. The distinctiveness and remarkability demanded by Lynch's notion of imageability means that an object may at first appear a visual misfit, yet fits well when judged against less obvious factors. This has been framed as a continuum between understated and overstated intentions (Harland 2015b: 94), the former being good fit and the latter less so in visual terms.

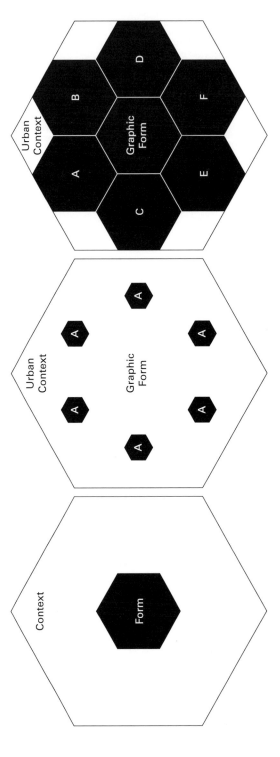

1. GOODNESS OF FIT
'Rightness' of form happens when the relationship between form and context is harmonious. Appropriateness determines the degree to which the form fits the rest of the ensemble.

2. CITY OF WESTMINSTER
In the case of the City of Westminster street nameplate, the same graphic form is dispersed throughout the borough. This identifies each road and reinforces the district identity at regular intervals.

3. KABUKICHŌ
In the case of the Kabukicho, different graphic forms are so compact that the density unifies to provide one of the defining images of Tokyo: the 'electric street'. Graphic form saturates the urban context.

FIGURE 5.1 *Ensembles of form and context.*

Alexander's explanation of form and context applied to the City of Westminster street nameplate and the dense illuminated signs of Kabukichō, Shinjuku.

So often, graphic objects must stand out from their context, especially to meet commercial objectives, as is often the case with fast food restaurant fasciae. For example, the brash red, white and yellow fascia of McDonald's became ubiquitous in the late twentieth century, emblazoning the world's urban environments. For McDonald's, this represented good fit with their globalization strategy. Yet some considered it a misfit with local visual–aesthetic priorities. For example, in 1986 McDonald's opened their 'il primo ristorante' in Rome's Piazza di Spagna (one of its most historic squares) but local resistance determined that McDonald's install a discreet fascia sign barely noticeable from the opposite side of the piazza. The fascia colour in bronze was sympathetic to the building's façade. Compared to the more sedate nameplate that identifies the piazza, it stands out, but the wider perspective sees it recede into the building's façade, ironically allowing a garish regulatory 'No Entry' sign to take precedence. Furthermore, in close proximity a number of strategically placed McDonald's direction signs in the familiar red, white and yellow announce you are in the vicinity of the restaurant. Here, in the case of McDonald's, fit defies misfit by introducing heritage concerns to the mix. But such concerns are absent when looking across the piazza in the opposite direction, where the M of Metro interrupts the vista! See Plate 11.

The adaptation of the red, white and yellow McDonald's fascia responds to fit more sympathetically with the surrounding environment, which includes other graphic objects. It restores goodness of fit in an ensemble usually unacquainted with an historically sensitive context. The Piazza di Spagna context placed demands on the graphic form to adapt in a new ensemble, as illustrated in Figure 5.2.

The variables that determine good fit are infinite and we have concentrated on some that prompt visual–aesthetic considerations, focusing on objects that impact on our visual sense of place and graphic image of the city. The continuum between appropriateness and inappropriateness may be subtle or blatant. For example, two similar applications of inscription on public buildings respond differently to the degree of sunshine on the surface of the characters, and the degree of shadow that intrudes on legibility. Figure 5.3 shows the Tokyo Medical University Hospital inscription as a better fit than the Shibaura Institute of Technology inscription because the figure ground contrast is greater in the former – only part of the space within the Japanese characters is obscured due to shadow, and the Roman lettering reads in full. In the Shibaura Institute of Technology inscription, although the large Japanese characters benefit from the reflected sunlight, both the smaller characters and the Roman lettering are obscured by the greater contrast between the shadow and the background. In these cases, weather conditions, as part of fit, have not been taken fully into account.

The interchange between form and context in an ensemble explains in part why and how objects look as they do. Whereas we have previously referred to objects that demonstrate some form of graphic address, we have not yet been able to frame this as a system in itself, related to other systems. This is what Alexander does when he refers to form as a pattern or system. Urban graphic objects are also pattern, and function not only as graphic language but also pattern language.

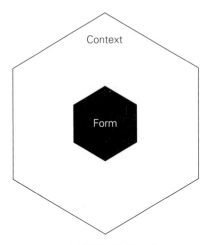

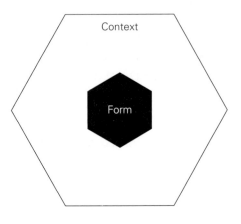

1. GOODNESS OF FIT
'Rightness' of form happens when the relationship between form and context is harmonious. Appropriateness determines the degree to which the form fits the rest of the ensemble.

2. MISFIT
'Wrongness' of form happens when the context changes and form no longer fits the context. Then, inappropriateness leads to difficulty in understanding how form fits with the rest of the ensemble.

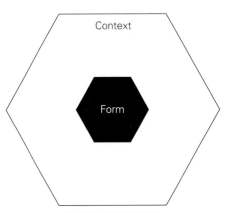

3. NEW ENSEMBLE
As issues emerge that place new demands on form, 'rightness' is restored by adapting the form to changes in context. Appropriateness continues to determine the degree to which the form fits the rest of the ensemble.

FIGURE 5.2 *Evolving goodness of fit to a new ensemble.*

As new problems emerge associated with context, if the form does not adapt then misfit occurs. Restoring rightness happens when form changes to align with context in a new ensemble.

FIGURE 5.3 *The impact of weather on type form (Tokyo, Japan 2013)*

Neither of these building inscriptions fully considers how daylight and sunshine may cast unwanted shadow. The Tokyo Medical University Hospital is closer to 'good fit' in that there is better figure-ground contrast, but the Shibaura Institute of Technology inscription is more of a misfit.

Object as pattern

'Pattern' invariably means regular form, design, plan, prototype, or regularity. Alexander *et al.* (1977) use the word to define a form or system that solves design problems. These are solutions to problems in all urban places, and they propose 253 patterns that, together, form a pattern language and intelligible portrayal of a region. At the largest scale, a pattern comprises an independent region or the distribution of towns compared to the smallest pattern detailing the personal things we surround ourselves with in the home. Thus, and drawing from ideas explored in Chapter 4, a pattern is an entity connected to other patterns in a macro–meso–micro structure that may represent a part or a whole.

Urban graphic objects conform to this description but are unaccounted for in Alexander *et al.*'s explanation of what pattern language is. Only 'Road Crossing' and 'Ornament' resemble anything aligned to our intentions here. These are at either end of a spectrum that, according to certain criteria, determines whether or not a pattern is successful. Each of the 253 patterns is marked with two asterisks, one asterisk, or no asterisk (two being the most successful and none not having succeeded and in need of alternative solutions). In their estimation of the design problems associated with a road crossing (no asterisk) their recommendation does not succeed, whereas their assessment of ornamentation (two asterisks) is that it is 'a deep and inescapable property of a well-formed environment' (1977: xiv).

Accompanying each pattern is an archetypal photograph of the system. The road-crossing photograph features the familiar arrangement of elongated white rectangles (metaphorically called a 'zebra crossing' in the UK). Ornament is depicted as large star shapes on a two-storey domestic building exterior with abstract window surrounds.

In discussion about the visual dimension of urban design Carmona *et al.* (2010) overlook the ubiquitous road crossing, and ornamentation is implicit in the discussion about façade design and floorscape, yet these are two of the more obvious examples of graphic form in the urban context and deserving of closer attention. In order to substantiate both, we next discuss how the visual symbolism associated with crossing the road has since acquired heightened recognition, and how ornamentation is more than something to adorn a building. Both examples focus on 'hard' floorscape, but illustrate more than the simple arrangement and inter-relation with other materials and landscape features. They have become part of our urban visual culture.

The road (zebra) crossing

Alexander *et al.* (1977) define the problem associated with road crossing as the contrast between the physical differences between cars, their weight, speed and potential to fail, compared to people. 'No amount of painted white lines, crosswalks, traffic lights, button operated signals, ever quite manage to change the fact that a car weighs a ton or more, and will run over any pedestrian, unless the driver brakes' (1977: 281). The proposed solution – acknowledged by them as 'extraordinary' and unsatisfactory – is to make a 'knuckle' on either side of the road and narrow the lanes to a single car width in each direction, adding an island in-between. Furthermore, the proposal is to raise the pedestrian crossing by 12 inches above the road surface, sloping the road up to that level at an incline of 1:6 and increasing visibility by erecting a canopy or shelter. They profess this should only be done where 'badly needed' and allude specifically to wide roads with several lanes that are impassable. Evidence suggests that few places have implemented this in the decades since.

Yet, the abundance of painted white rectangles in megacities such as Tokyo and São Paulo, and at the intricate junctions of Parisian streets, suggest a graphic solution has become the norm. These are embedded in the mental image and symbolism people associate with crossing the road, to the point where they are prepared to enact their own interventions and paint their own white rectangles where necessary. For example, on Thursday 11 July 2013, a headline appeared in a local newspaper reading 'Fake zebra crossing painted on busy street' (O'Pray 2013). The story featured a photograph taken by a local resident showing five white rectangles and five incomplete white rectangle outlines painted onto the carriageway, and a person walking across from one side to the other. The 'do-it-yourself' crossing was accompanied by a sign reading 'School children crossing weekdays 8.40am to 9am', emphasizing the need to draw attention to child safety due to the close proximity of a nearby primary school for children aged 11 and under. The white rectangles were hastily painted out the next day because, as stated in the article, it is an offence to paint on the carriageway. Aside from this moment of design activism by a local person, it exemplifies the values associated with the 'zebra crossing' as a safe place to cross, where form and context are understood and customs observed.

As suggested by the thought experiment at the beginning of Chapter 3, the zebra crossing is an image simple enough for a member of the public to paint at full size. It is a ubiquitous graphic image of the city, and the most visible defining form in Alexander *et al.*'s archetypal road crossing pattern photograph. Yet they trivialize the white lines, traffic lights, and button operated signals in favour of a physical intervention involving elevating the road surface at the point of crossing, with the intention of forcing cars to slow down. These days, considering the number of pedestrian points in cities such as Tokyo or Paris, the recommendations are unfeasible.

The zebra crossing (so called by the UK Prime Minister Jim Callaghan in the 1970s) in its basic visual form is most recognizable by the parallel longitudinal stripes that cross a carriageway. Usually painted white onto the road surface, it may occasionally be in other colour combinations, depending on the context. It signifies a safe place to cross and aspires to give priority to pedestrians as well as to warn motorists. The crossing has been a feature of the urban environment since the British Government's

Road Research Laboratory (RRL) designed it in the late 1940s. Reports suggest it was initially installed in 1,000 locations in 1949 before nationwide implementation in 1951, but soon after was adopted worldwide and has since been adapted for use in airports, car parks and inside buildings amongst other applications. The sequence of white rectangles, usually arranged with equal gaps in between is synonymous and extensive from the world's major capital cities to small villages, found in most settlement types in one form or other, with the probable exceptions being isolated settlements and hamlets.

Its appearance is regulated in the UK through a basic diagram that determines its application. See Plate 17. This details not only the black and white rectangular stripes that characterize its name but also short lines that define the 'give way' position and a concertina of other lines, the use of studs and the familiar pole-mounted orange globe on either side of the road. See Plate 18. In other places, such as Tokyo and São Paulo, additional graphic elements suspended above the crossing provide additional signals to the driver. See Plate 19. Application in the UK generally conforms closely to the diagram, even though the regulations allow a number of permissible variations. Deviation is more evident worldwide, where the arrangement of elements have adjusted to suit local conditions. See Plate 20. The constant feature is the black and white stripes that signify road crossing to pedestrians, cyclists and vehicles, no matter how temporary, irregular and inappropriately placed. See Plate 21. The scope of implementation is large: the device must cope with the tough demands of a busy intersection, such as New York's Times Square; extensions in width rather than length across the carriageway; irregular shapes that cover a junction in the entirety; white rectangles combined with black when appearing on a muted surface; and in combination with other graphic devices. When not maintained, painted versions often diminish to appear as a 'ghost' crossing. But when integrated within hard floorscape in contrasting material, the durability is a good fit with the local setting. See Plate 22. The Avenue des Champs-Élysées is a good example of this, where, at the Arc de Triomphe, the wide sidewalks integrate understated versions of the basic pattern. In contrast, the Avenue's road surface favours durable white painted crossings as part of three concentric 'collars' that circumnavigate the Arc de Triomphe. See Plate 23.

In the UK, opinions about the effectiveness of the zebra crossing have varied over time. Some argue that throughout its period of use it has saved lives and has been an invaluable contribution to road safety. More recently, however, the number of deaths is said to have increased due to the reluctance of drivers to stop in the absence of a red light. Consequently, white stripes alone are now thought to be insufficient. Throughout its life there has been an increase in additional graphic devices to influence pedestrian behaviour. In 1934, pole-mounted orange spheres and metal studs were enough to indicate pedestrian crossings in the UK, but the studs were deemed imperceptible to motorists. Consequently, the Ministry of Transport experimented with blue-and-yellow and red-and-white stripes, eventually deciding on the black-and-white stripes, measuring 40–60 cm wide.

Paradoxically, coloured variations are used in other countries such as Italy. See Plate 24. Alternatively, the white stripes have been combined with other floor surface colours that delineate other uses. See Plate 25. Nevertheless, some landscape architecture appears to completely integrate the device into the carriageway design, complying with the geometry of an overall junction layout or crossing point. See Plate 26. Such careful placement may also be integrated within an urban design development, and provides a welcome focal point in an otherwise indifferent setting. In such instances, additional graphic elements also add a human presence. See Plate 27. Although these schemes seemingly integrate the crossing into the floorscape with precision, the pedestrian's transition from sidewalk to street may also be enhanced by the consistent or similar use of patterns for both surfaces. See Plate 28. Whereas, in other locations where safety and security may be more paramount, the distinctiveness of the white (and black) alternating rectangles will need to provoke greater awareness amongst pedestrians, especially where people are travelling in groups with small children. See Plate 29.

However, the function of a road crossing is no longer only to assist people in getting from A to B with a modicum of safety and security. The zebra crossing has become a cultural landmark. The Beatles walked on it for their *Abbey Road* album cover (see Plate 30); activists stencilled on it in Paris with poetic quotations (Anon 1997: 14); it's a location in motion pictures such as *Babel*; and is one of Tokyo's top tourist attractions where the constraining lines do little to control pedestrians at the Shibuya Crossing. See Plate 31.

Painted white rectangles across the floorscape have become synonymous with the idea of road (pedestrian) crossing. It is first and foremost a graphic solution, a graphic element and city element embedded in the mind of people to such an extent that they see it as a solution to more than the problem of speeding cars. It has become such an everyday part of urban visual culture that some feel motivated enough to draw their own versions on the carriageway where they think it necessary, if only then to have it painted out! See Plate 32.

Ornamentation (as Unification)

Alexander *et al.* (1977: 1147) define the 'problem' associated with ornamentation as the instinct people have to decorate their surroundings. This is one of the patterns that meet the two-asterisk standard, meaning it is a fundamental pattern language. Their recommendation is to emphasize transitions and edges with decoration using simple repetitive themes that unify otherwise separate entities. The principle is represented in two basic diagrams placed side-by-side. On the left are two adjacent upright rectangles with a narrow cleavage in between. Next to this is the same arrangement but across the cleavage a single overlapping heart shape is cut into each rectangle in a symmetrical layout. The heart assumes the focus of attention, its shape communicating an act of unification. The sentiment is easily understood because it is an identifiable image for millions of people – a heart stands for love. The accompanying text explains that 'the main purpose of ornament in the environment – in buildings, rooms, and public spaces – is to make the world more whole . . .' (Alexander *et al.* 1977: 1147).

Ornamentation as an act of unification is different in purpose to the way a street nameplate accomplishes the same – it is less concerned with imparting information and more with the pleasure associated with decoration. We have seen how the City of Westminster strives for unification with a small but strategically positioned street nameplates, and how Kabukichō's illuminations blend into a single rhetorical fuse covering a smaller area but with greater chaotic intensity. Ornamentation also has the same capacity to unify an area, and floorscape is one way to achieve this. Floorscape graphics not only communicate a place to cross the road, or outline a playing surface for sport, but also reflect the spatial relations and complicated histories in the aesthetic component of what visual culture scholars refer to as 'visuality' (Mirzoeff 2013: xxxi). The city centres of Lisbon and São Paulo exemplify this.

The floorscapes of Lisbon and São Paulo display the same cobbled surface in ornate patterns and motifs. See Plate 12. In Lisbon, the distinctive patterns (also used as pedestrian crossings and car and bus lanes markings) extensively contribute to the whole pedestrian, tram and motorcar user experience, informing the city image with contrasting black and white configurations. In São Paulo, specifically around its historic centre, the same material approach is especially pertinent as it represents the colonial past between Portugal and Brazil. Similar patterns also exist in other places with close colonial links to Portugal, such as Macau.

As a graphic language, the technique and visual–aesthetic appeal represents the political structures and economic and cultural relationships between Portugal and Brazil that date back to the age of colonialism in the fifteenth century, when European powers led by Spain and Portugal expanded into Africa, Asia and the New World. Portugal discovered Brazil in 1500 and colonization happened some 30 years later. Since then – in a predominantly Spanish-speaking continent – Brazil has maintained its Portuguese connection. This is most obviously represented through spoken language, but the relationship is also signified in the decorative floorscape patterns found in the urban centres of both countries.

On the world stage, the floorscape pattern is constantly associated with the well-known Copacabana Beach in Rio de Janeiro, where the wide patterned walkway divides the beach and road. It contributes to one of the most identifiable images of Brazil and was used as a key location-defining image in coverage of the 2014 World Cup, transferring its purpose from ornamentation to place identity and promotion. When we need to promote the essence of Brazil for commercial benefit, floorscape is one of the images that comes to mind, even though the pattern is quintessentially Portuguese. See Figure 5.4.

FIGURE 5.4 *Malibu meets Copacabana Beach in Scandinavia (Umeå, Sweden 2014).*

This promotion for the liqueur 'Malibu' is via Copacabana Beach in a Scandinavian Airport with an accompanying Portuguese floorscape.

Summary

In this chapter, urban graphic objects have been positioned in relation to more recent thinking about the visual dimension of urban design, and particularly the visual–aesthetic aspect. Within this, the relationship between form and context has been explained, and the pattern and aesthetic order that features prominently in the visual dimension of urban design has been traced back to earlier explanations of pattern language, and earlier again to the relationship between form and context in design. We have seen how the fallible patterns that contribute to pattern language are in need of new perspectives that place higher value on symbolic meaning than physical infrastructure – the road crossing being a blatant example – and how fundamental patterns such as ornamentation adapt to perform more than one function and come to represent more than adornment. Ornamental images also migrate and assume different meanings. There is clearly a wider set of functions that graphic objects satisfy beyond an inclination to gratify, and this will be the objective of the next chapter – to clarify what is the purpose of urban graphic objects as a form of representation.

6

Representamen

The Sign can only represent the Object and tell about it.

PEIRCE, IN BUCHLER 1955: 100

Introduction

Chapter 6 begins a process of formulating urban graphic objects into some kind of typology to match what has been done in urban design. More than before in this book, it consciously casts, or superimposes, a graphic design stance over three of four known types at the core of urban design. To have done this sooner without the various theoretical perspectives would have been to overlook useful concepts which provide the basis for this chapter. These perspectives, other than graphic design, will not be covered extensively but enough to help establish a basic theory of graphic objects in urban objects. What emerges in this chapter, evidenced through the photo-documentation consistent with previous chapters, is how the products of graphic design form a layer of urban design to facilitate much of the way people interact with environments.

This chapter asks questions about how language should be used to explain urban graphic phenomena. From the perspective of graphic design, the current discourse is much less than satisfactory because of the multiple meanings associated with certain words such as image and sign (and object). While these words facilitate theoretical discourse, they hinder the transfer of ideas into practice and the development of graphic design into a wider community of practice and more serious academic pursuit. Interdisciplinary discourse is not helped by the ambiguity associated with same word usage. For example, not even semioticians are consistent or appear comfortable with the use of the word sign in a theory of signs.

The main aim of this chapter is, therefore, to start to bridge the gap between type (in the type design sense) and typology (in the urban design sense) and to lay the foundations for establishing a better understanding of the products of graphic design and the nature of urban design.

From typography towards typology

We have previously discussed how the design of a page provided an analogy for understanding city design and real space. In a similar vein, the study of printing fonts provides us with the word *typology*, meaning classification or categorization and metaphor for organizational systems. The first known use of typology in 1845 came in the middle of a century of technological change that encouraged the creation of an unlimited number of typefaces and the gradual acknowledged importance and specialism of typographic design and design of books, as opposed to an activity previously undertaken by compositors and craftsmen, for example in Britain and America. Typology came after the word *stereotype*, coined in 1798 to represent 'a plate cast from a mould of a surface of type' (Leyens *et al.* 1994: 9). Now, typology is used in many disciplines such as anthropology, archaeology, linguistics, psychology, theology, statistics, urban planning and architecture, all stemming from graphic representation. Although underutilized in graphic design, classifying and describing typefaces has continued since the advent of typeface categorization in the nineteenth century and the 'massive expansion' of typeface range (Baines and Haslam 2005: 50).

Lang (2005: xxii) explains that the 'classification of examples enables designers to refer to processes and products that might be of use in informing them about the situation they face and the possible ways of dealing with it'. We have seen in the previous chapter and noted earlier what little information is available to help urban designers deal with graphic communication problems, and we have discovered that this is generally overlooked in the visual–aesthetic dimension of urban design. Nor does graphic language feature in a pattern language for towns, buildings and construction. Earlier in this book alphabets, typography, images, tools and disciplines were flagged up as the anatomy of graphic design, and elements, goals and effects were listed as activities, but these are not framed as typology, category or classification in such a way that the urban designer might adopt and adapt for use in the different types of urban design. Questions therefore arise about the classification of graphic objects for use in urban design, but as graphic design is such an eclectic field it is difficult to know where to start.

The *image* in imageability is as good a place as any. The notion of image is prominent in contemporary life as entertainment, information, advertising, journalism, television, internet, films, computer games, fascias, print, instructions, tourism, catalogues, identity, brands, cosmetics, fashion, and more. But to Lynch, image meant a mental image. In graphic design, it more often means something concrete, such as a photograph or illustration. Graphic designers talk about imagemaking (i.e. the making of images in the physical sense). Yet variations in the use of the word have been differentiated in the field of critical theory and aesthetics through five categories under a definition that interprets images as 'likeness', 'resemblance' and 'similitude':

Graphic: pictures, statues, designs
Optical: mirrors, projections
Perceptual: sense data, 'species', appearances
Mental: dreams, memories, ideas, fantasmata
Verbal: metaphors, descriptions

MITCHELL 1986: 10

Within these categories, derived from across the science-humanities spectrum, distinctions are clear and graphic images are the most concrete, but this interpretation of graphic image is derived mainly from the work of art historians.

Elkins (1999: 82) evolves this further by analysing one-, two- and three-part domains for the image: image, word/image, and writing/picture/notation combinations, leading on to a further seven-part structure of allography/semasiography/pseudowriting/subgraphemic/hypographemic/emblemata/schemata. This supports a view that the vast array of visual images are not art, or 'nonart' images, but should be more appropriately located within the Greek word 'gramma' ('picture, written letter, and piece of writing') or by the verb 'graphien' ('write, draw, or scratch') to accommodate breadth. The argument is that these terms are more appropriate than 'image', 'visual artefact', 'text', 'writing', or the combined 'word and image', 'pictures, writing and notation' and that the largest set of objects under this category should be more aptly referred to under the rubric of 'graphism'. Pictures, statues and designs are a partial portrayal of what a graphic image is, and design provides enough justification for our purpose here to seek solace in the notion of the graphic image. However, classification is clearly problematic to the extent that some of those who study images think it a pointless pursuit. 'Images thus constitute a problematic field for contemporary intellectual endeavour' and some think that to delineate the fundamental nature of image as 'futile' (Manghani *et al.* 2006: 3).

The lack of a general image classification system, and the use of image as both a physical and mental construct, thwarts a better understanding of graphic design as urban design through Lynch's notion of imageability, similar to the way sign assumes different meanings across disciplines. This is evident when cultural theorists talk about how meaning is produced and exchanged through representation as language, signs and images (Hall 1997: 15). Consistent with our earlier discussion, 'signs' in this instance is explained as a general term for words, sounds or images, organized into 'languages' which also, in the very broad sense, stand for facial expression, gesture, fashion, or traffic lights. The critical crux of this scenario of the 'sign' is that representation is dependent on both 'verbal' and 'visual' form as likeness described and depicted. Furthermore, representation means symbolization in the same way metaphor works. Hall (1997: 1–19) defines this as two systems of representation that associate objects, people and events in the world with what he invariably refers to as concepts, ideas, thoughts and feelings in our mind, transferred through 'signs' organized into languages (words, sounds or images) – image at first being equal to language as well as part of it.

Confusion is further enforced when Hall states 'Visual signs and images, even when they bear a close resemblance to the things to which they refer, are still signs: they carry meaning and thus have to be interpreted' (1997: 19). Visual signs here are clearly different from verbal signs, but the earlier concerns with the dual meaning of sign remain as the semiotic sign assumes greater importance. The time has come to investigate the source of this dichotomy.

The semiotic sign

In the relationship between communication, meaning and signs, semiotics determines that signs are recognized as the components constituting a message. The basic concept is that a sign is an intermediate device between a user and a thing it directs attention to. What, then, is a semiotic sign?

In semiotics, also known as semiology, the two dominant models come from the American philosopher C. S. Peirce, who developed a triadic model encompassing the sign, the user and the object, and the Swiss linguist Ferdinand de Saussure who concentrated on a unified signifier and signified relationship, one pointing towards the other. Hence, although the same field, semiotics stands for the American branch, whereas semiology represents the European tradition.

Peirce's model is comprised of three components – sign (or as Peirce also stated – representamen), object and interpretent – and these work, interdependently. Often configured in a triangular diagram with three double-headed arrows pointing each way between the three components, Chandler (2007: 29) suggests that Peirce did not use such simplistic visualizations to convey the relationship between the three. However, in 1908, Peirce did depict the object, interpretent and sign in a diagrammatic model of 10 classes of sign (Queiroz and Farias 2014: 527). Nevertheless, the components have been explained as:

1   The representamen : the form which the sign takes (not necessarily material, though usually interpreted as such) – called by some theorists the 'sign vehicle'.
2   An interpretant : not an interpreter but rather the sense made of the sign.
3   An object : something beyond the sign to which it refers (a referent).

CHANDLER 2007: 29

Sign, in the Peirce sense, combines all of these rather than sign meaning only a material thing such as a road sign or shop fascia. All three are essential in that the sign is the unity of what is being referred to (the object, or the referent), how it is represented (representamen) and how it is interpreted (the interpretant). But Peirce's explanation is at times confusing as he refers to a first and second priority for sign such as when he states that a 'sign' is 'something which stands to somebody for something in some respect or capacity' and 'it addresses somebody, that is, creates in the mind of that person an equivalent sign, or perhaps a more developed sign. That sign which it creates I call the *interpretant* of the first sign', and further aligns sign to both external and internal phenomena in stating 'A *Sign* is a Representamen with a mental Interpretant' (Buchler 1955: 99–100, original italic). By comparison, de Saussure's linguistic bias defined sign as a 'concept (signified)' and 'sound pattern (signifier)' (similar to 'sign vehicle'), although sound pattern did not actually mean something physical, more psychological, and material only in the sense of a representation of 'sensory impressions' (de Saussure, (1983: 66) cited in Chandler 2007: 14).

Moreover, de Saussure's model does not directly account directly for what Peirce called *representamen*. 'Sign', in the de Saussure sense, stands for the immaterial psychological connection between signified and signifier. 'The linguistic sign unites not a thing and a name, but a concept and a sound-image. The latter is not the material sound, a purely physical thing, but a psychological imprint of the sound, the impression that it makes on our senses' (de Saussure 1915: 66). For example, Barnard uses the example of a traffic sign and states the red light is the signifier associated with the concept 'stop' which acts as the signified (Barnard 2005: 26). In short, de Saussure argues for the linguistic sign as a dual psychological entity; he represents this in a drawing of an oval shape split in half by a horizontal line. Above the line is the word concept (signified); below is the word sound-image (signifier), with an arrow on either side, one pointing up and the other down. The unity of the two is assumed by the word sign for the whole, on the basis that de Saussure did not know of a better word (1915: 67).

In both Peirce and de Saussure's work, the word sign is used to represent a unity of things not necessarily material. In Peirce's model the word representamen more usefully serves the purpose of directing attention to and from the object, and to and from the interpretant. Both Peirce and de Saussure were inconsistent in the way they used the word sign to stand for unity, and the importance they each attach to the word sign is less than might be expected. Peirce substituted one for the other, as in 'A *sign*, or *representamen* . . .' (Buchler 1955: 99) and de Saussure acknowledged difficulty with the word sign even though he chose to retain it for the unity of signified and signifier as much for ignorance than anything else (1915: 67). Consequently, semioticians distinguish between 'sign' and 'sign vehicle' (as signifier or representamen) confirming that de Saussure sometimes used sign when he meant signifier and Peirce used sign to mean representamen.

Of the two, Peirce detailed a typology of signs based on three orders of sign. These were *icon*, *index* and *symbol*, suggesting a sign is usually one of these. The basic difference between the three is that in an icon, resemblance is vital between the representamen and the object, for example, a photograph of the Empire State Building is an icon. An index is determined by causal effect, for example, a shadow indicating the sun shining. Whereas in a symbol the relationship between representamen and object is arbitrary (it will not necessarily possess any similarities) and must be amenable, that is to say it must be socially acceptable and agreeable from interpretant perspectives. For example, from our earlier discussions, the convention that the Empire State inscription stands for Empire State Building is agreed, even though there is no resemblance between the representamen and object. For further understanding, Chandler (2007a: 36–7) provides a list of examples for each sign mode:

- *Iconic*: a portrait, a cartoon, a scale-model, onomatopoeia, metaphors, realistic sounds in 'programme music', sound effects in radio drama, a dubbed film soundtrack, imitative gestures.

- *Indexical*: 'natural signs' (smoke, thunder, footprints, echoes, non-synthetic odours and flavours), medical symptoms (pain, a rash, pulse-rate), measuring instruments (weathercock, thermometer, clock, spirit-level), 'signals' (a knock on a door, a phone ringing), pointers (a pointing 'index' finger, a directional signpost), recordings (a photograph, a film, video or television shot, an audio-recorded voice), personal 'trademarks' (handwriting, catch-phrases).

- *Symbolic*: language in general (plus specific languages, alphabetical letters, punctuation marks, words, phrases and sentences), numbers, morse code, traffic lights, national flags.

Graphic design employs all of these modes, often in a single object whereby signs gain in meaning from the close association with other signs in a syntagmatic relationship, or in a paradigmatic sense when there is a clear contrast with other signs. Thus icon, index and symbol can be used to analyse the communication structure in graphic objects. Semiotic signs are complex, as there are often several signs working in tandem. An example will help to illustrate this.

Consider the packaging of long playing vinyl records in the second half of the twentieth century. These were sold in elaborately designed printed covers for protection and promotion. Some of the most recognizable examples were produced for The Beatles; their Abbey Road album being a case in point. See Plate 30. As their penultimate album (though last to be recorded) such was their fame that the cover has no band name or album title, just a photograph of the band members walking across a pedestrian crossing on a North London road, with a Volkswagen Beetle nearby. The band and road name, with the song titles, are on the reverse. The photograph faithfully portrays the band members as they looked in 1969. It's iconic. They chose to cross the road at the nearby pedestrian crossing. This aspect of the photograph is indexical, but so is the whole photograph in that it represents their last set of studio-recorded songs with such familiar songs as *Come Together*, *Something*, or *Here Comes the Sun*. If you wanted to listen to one of these songs in the late twentieth century, you most likely selected the album from your record collection. It's a signifier of their final compilation of studio songs.

The crossing is also a symbol, in that this particular configuration of white rectangles on the carriageway is an agreed code for a safe place to cross the road. We may ask further questions such as why Paul McCartney is barefoot. Four possible answers to this are proffered; he had no shoes with him that day (iconic), it was a hot day (indexical), it reflects Paul's penchant for a gimmick (also indexical); it's a Mafia sign of death (symbolic) and implied to some Americans he was dead (Roylance *et al.* 2000: 341–2).

In semiotics, the object is called the referant. In the case of the Abbey Road album cover, the object to which it refers is that particular set of Beatles songs. Conversely, in our discussion about urban graphic objects, we have been arguing for representamen as object in the concrete sense, more so than signifier as a psychological impression and a representation as a sensory impression. It is not proposed here that we collapse these two aspects of Peirce's triadic model, but there is clearly a conflict in language use with two meanings associated with the word object. With this in mind, the question of representamen in the material sense, as concrete object, needs to be explored if we are to acknowledge graphic objects beyond being semiotic signs.

Object as representamen

In semiotics, representamen points to an object and, so far, we have preferred to favour the physical. Representation as a mental faculty is dependent on the process of assimilating a new idea with the existing ideas. Kant uses the example of a triangle:

> . . . we think of a triangle as an object by being conscious of the combination of three straight lines according to a rule by which such an intuition can always be presented. This unity of rule determines all the manifold, and limits it to conditions which render the unity of apperception possible; and the concept of this unity is the representation of the object = X . . .

> 2007 [1781]: 136

More than making sense of an idea, we discussed earlier how representation expresses the thoughts, concepts, ideas or feelings as external things: as language, as sign, as image (Hall 1997: 1–30). Each possessed a material quality, in the same sense that a physicist might argue, does speech. For the purpose of our discussion, material refers to something that can be experienced and has been produced by the craftsman, the engineer, and the scientist.

It will be clear by now that explaining representation by using words such as object or image is problematic in an inter-disciplinary context. Difficulty exists in the process of selecting words that could occupy either the mental or material domain, as many are interchangeably used in mental/material or outside/inside discussion. Similarly, words such as 'thing' might equally stand for an inanimate object, action, event, thought or utterance, whereby an object is something external. An example of this can be drawn from Kant, who explains how representations establish a concept. He discusses the relationship between intuition and object by expounding how intuition happens through sensibility in receipt of objects, which once thought through, provides understanding that leads on to concepts. He goes on to say:

> The effect produced by an object upon the capacity for representation, insofar as we are affected by the object, is sensation. An intuition that refers to an object through sensation is called empirical. The undetermined object of an empirical intuition is called appearance.
>
> That in an appearance which corresponds to sensation I call its matter; but that which brings about the fact that the manifold of the appearance can be ordered in certain relations, I call the form of appearance ... Now, that in which alone sensations can be ordered and placed in a certain form cannot be sensation again. Consequently, despite the fact that the matter of all appearance is given to us only *a posteriori*, its form must lie ready for the sensations *a priori* in the mind, and must therefore allow of being considered apart from all sensation.

KANT 2007 [1781]: 59, original italics

In this passage he is suggesting mind and object are separate, and sensibility is the entry point through which an object must pass in order to be intuited and thought about. Objects are given to us through sensibility, and intuition makes this instantaneous. This leads to thought and the development of concepts that, in turn, are part of intuition and sensibility. That said, the word *object* to describe things external and physical is also contested by Kant. 'We may indeed call everything insofar as we are conscious of it, an object; but it requires a more profound investigation to discover what this word may mean with regard to appearances, not insofar as they (as representations) are objects, but insofar as they only signify an object' (2007 [1781]: 213). He refers to the *transcendental object* as being known to neither as inner or outer intuition, but the *empirical object* is the former 'if represented only in a relation of time' and the latter 'if it is represented in space', suggesting *empirically external* objects are outside of us. This clearly reinforces the earlier proposition that urban graphic objects are fundamentally spatial. 'Kant sees that when it comes to space and time, size, shape, and the objective order, to have a concept is not to have a mental picture. It is to have an organizing principle or rule; a way of handling the flux of data' (Blackburn 1999: 255–6). This highlights a critical distinction between an object that is deduced from experience, say as a resemblance or picture, and one that is determined by thought categories.

Based on Kant's explanation, Figure 6.1 attempts to show how the empirically external object is given to us through sensibility, and via intuition (feeling), thought, concept, and ideas. It is determined as empirical through the 'effect' of sensation. Sensibility and sensation appear to operate at the threshold between the internal mental and external material systems of representation. A cube is used to illustrate this. Depicted is the idea of a cube (a six-sided three-dimensional shape made up of equal proportions arranged symmetrically); how one might conceive of a cube (in

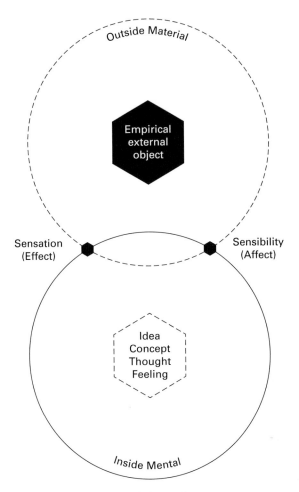

FIGURE 6.1 *Representation through sensibility and sensation.*

relation to other objects); think about a cube (in terms of what it might be used for, for example, dice); and what emotions a cube might invoke (e.g. a building, or the role of dice).

In semiotics, the object is the referant. We are concerned in this book with the object as representamen. Kant provides us with an understanding of how the object as representamen is understood through sensation (or what might be called effect) and sensibility. To study the nature of something is to be concerned with its basic or inherent features, character, or quality as phenomena. The phenomena of graphic objects within the urban object is treated here as a schema, meaning a 'systematic . . . unity of manifold kinds of knowledge under one idea', or 'architectonic' (Kant 2007 [1781]: 652–3). As suggested earlier, it also aspires to be a pattern.

Having reviewed the way semioticians use the word sign and argued for object as representamen in the material sense, we have established three different kinds of sign as icon, index and symbol. Furthermore, having argued for object as representamen and therefore object as icon, index and symbol, we have been able to identify three types of sign, but without any understanding of their purpose. What else does an icon, index or symbol do? What is the function of graphic objects?

The function of graphic objects

Earlier, we discussed how Alexander depicted ornamentation using a heart device between two upright rectangles. This demonstrated the potential of a simple model for applying the principle of scale to graphic objects as urban objects. It illustrated how two distinct entities, functioning individually, could unite through the addition of a heart as a representation of ornamentation. This principle of mediation through ornamentation as a pattern language, whilst appropriate to a discussion about graphic objects, is also limited in scope for our purpose here. Most of the examples featured in this book would be inappropriately defined as ornaments, though they may possess ornamental qualities. For example, the Empire State Building inscription conveys information, but in an ornamental way; the Trajan's Column inscription displays serifs derived from the master letterer's use of a brush, but a modern typeface such as Times New Roman retains these for little more than ornamentation purposes. However, Alexander's ornamentation pattern may be extended to accommodate an understanding of the wider functions of graphic design.

Graphic objects fulfil a wide range of functions, not least social, cultural and economic functions, but these are not our concern here. Instead, we are interested in the individual functions of graphic objects. Many adjectives have been used to describe the purpose of graphic design: identification, information, presentation and promotion, referential, emotive, connotative, poetic/aesthetic, meta-linguistic, phatic, persuasion, education, administration, decorative, magic, representation, orientation and systematic (van der Waarde 2009: 23). Some of these, notably identification, aesthetics, decoration, representation, orientation and systematic, have already been covered in this book so far.

Barnard (2005) has focused on six functions and these will suffice to explain the purpose of individual graphic objects in the built environment. According to Barnard, these account for all graphic production. However, he cautions that these functions do not perform alone; most objects will serve more than one function. However, it is possible to identify some functions as being more prominent than another. For example, a road sign is designed more to communicate information and identification than to persuade and coerce, whereas a billboard advertisement does quite the opposite.

By Barnard's reckoning, the *information* function is to impart knowledge. Common urban objects such as pub signs, shop fronts, coats of arms, company logos, signage, diagrams, and maps are elementary examples. *Persuasion* performs a rhetorical function and seeks to affect behaviour typically through advertising, political propaganda or electoral publicity. Although these also satisfy the information function, the intention is attention-seeking as opposed to people-seeking information. *Decoration* does neither of these first two so directly as it is more concerned with elevating aesthetics, directed towards ornamentation or entertainment, leisure and pleasure, as noted in the earlier example of Lisbon's floorscape. The least palpable function is *magic*, whereby graphic design possesses qualities described by Barnard as sacred and transformative. By this he means the representation of something absent but with strong emotional connotations, as seen in the earlier example of the commemorative white crosses on Remembrance Sunday displayed in a public space. The magic function not only brings distant things close to us – the war dead in the case of Remembrance Sunday poppies – but also changes one thing into another. The last two – *metalinguistic* and *phatic* – Barnard groups together. The metalinguistic function satisfies a need to use one language to represent another in terms of explanation, clarification or qualification. This utilizes codes in the same way that a key on a map works, or an exclamation mark draws attention to something that does not quite make sense or needs to be treated with caution. Finally, phatic devices link or direct in the way an arrow works, or broken lines that indicate lanes on a highway. As noted above, none of these functions are independent from each other, but to reiterate, some functions are more apparent than others. For example, a stop sign is informative more than persuasive or decorative, directly linking a driver's actions to the environment in the way graphic devices link distinct entities. A commemorative cross in a graveyard might suggest access to the realm of the sacred in some transformative, magic-like, way. Or, coloured circles such as those on the New York subway, provide a metalinguistic key to using New York's subway network, while the white lines that determine the parking positions in a car park perform a phatic role.

This overview of graphic design's individual functions provides a framework for analysing the role of graphic objects in the urban object. If transposed onto the functions of cities and urban places – communications, economic, cognitive and display – a structure for understanding the complexity of how a category of graphic objects influences behaviour in cities becomes plausible.

These functions, coupled with the way images have been explained and the different types of semiotic sign, begin to suggest different ways that graphic objects can be classified into a typology. This chapter has so far explored the importance of classification and some approaches have been discussed. Graphic images from art history gave us pictures, statues and designs, as well as the notion of graphism, to stand for all manner of pictures, writing, drawing, scratching, words, images, visual artefacts, text, diagrams etc. as much examples of non-art than art. From critical theory, the picture, pictogram, ideogram and phonetic sign (Mitchell 1986: 27) help us to understand how new categories have developed over time. Other fields, such as cultural studies, offered representation as a more abstract approach whereby concepts, ideas, thoughts and

LIVERPOOL JOHN MOORES UNIVERSITY
LEARNING SERVICES

feelings are expressed through a clumsy combination of language, signs and images, language being heralded as words, sounds or images. This leads to the field of semiotics and the way a theory of signs encompasses the signified and signifier, as well as the form signs take (representamen), sign sense (interpretant), and what the sign refers to (object). In semiotics, or semiology, depending on whether you follow the Peirce or de Saussure tradition, their use of sign as a unifying concept, as well as a useful term for elaborating on their theories, hinders a fuller appreciation of what Peirce called representamen. (The same confusing problems were revealed in Lynch's work on the image of the city, whereby sign stood for more than sign!). However, Peirce's triadic relationship between representamen, interpretant, and referent affords the opportunity to treat representamen as the object, a graphic object, and the semiotic categorization of icon, index symbol explains what we earlier differentiated as sign and SIGN. Through Kant's interpretation of object as an external thing, given to us through sensibility and influencing us through sensation, we arrived at appearance, matter and form, and the empirical object as something represented in space. Furthermore, objects perform at least six different but inter-related functions – information, persuasion, decoration, magic, metalinguistic and phatic. This brief précis validates how difficult analysing urban graphic objects can be.

Missing from this list is a sense of the physical qualities that determine a graphic object. Line, shape, tone, colour, texture, form, scale, space and light all contribute in two, three and four dimensions, in static and dynamic states, but the possible permutations for categorizing graphic objects by their physical features would be an impossible task. Looking at specific elements that graphic designers use, such as lettering and typefaces, has been fruitful, but fails to acknowledge the point at which the object in question (lettering) moves beyond its alphabetic form and becomes more pictorial or diagrammatic. This is exemplified by a 'no entry' sign featuring a horizontal white line, or road works sign showing 'men at work'.

One might deduce from this that a graphic design stance is too difficult to define. There is no doubt that when individual graphic designers look at the environment, certain things attract the attention of one person that another will overlook. They do so with what was earlier phrased as a 'graphic eye'.

This book set out to establish graphic objects as urban objects through graphic design as urban design. The remaining case studies will explore how urban design functions through graphic objects. This will be undertaken by looking at the urban environment as three different types of urban design in order to show how an eclectic synthesis of graphic form serves as many needs as there are people. These examples – Ghirardelli Square in San Fancisco, La Défence near Paris and the Theater District and Times Square in New York – are drawn from case studies featured by Lang (2005) in his book *Urban Design: A Typology of Procedures and Products*. They map onto three of the four types of urban design work he suggests are at the core of urban design: all-of-a piece, piece-by-piece, and plug-in urban design (total urban design is omitted here on the basis that the other three are sufficient for illustrating the key issues). These types of urban design provide a manageable scale of urban units of analysis, offering sufficient scope to delineate a wide variety of graphic objects at work.

Ghirardelli Square, San Francisco (1962–7, 1982–4)

Judging by the number of empty retail units in 2013, Ghirardelli Square is no longer one of San Francisco's main tourist attractions. It is, however, a designated San Francisco Landmark recognised by the city's Historic Preservation Commission (formerly the Landmark Preservation Board) for its architectural and historical significance. This means any alterations to the building's fabric, as minor as replacing a sign for an ATM machine, must be compatible with the historic nature of the site in terms of design, materials, form, scale and location, with preservation, enhancement or restoration a priority (rather than damage or destruction). New components must match the existing aesthetic of the Romanesque Revival-style architecture, developed in three phases between 1864–1923.

Occupying a sloping block of land overlooking San Francisco Bay and Alcatraz, construction on the site began in 1864 with the Woollen Mill building by William A. Mooser, with additions in 1900 (Cocoa Building), 1911 (Chocolate and Mustard Building), 1915 (Power House), 1916 (Clock Tower and Apartment Building), 1919, (upper story of Chocolate Building), and 1923 (upper two stories of Cocoa Building), all by William A. Mooser II. These buildings remain and account for many of the identification signs at the complex today.

The factory complex was developed for chocolate making by the Ghirardelli family between 1900 and 1916, but is now a 'recycled' building complex. By the early 1960s, the site had fallen into disrepair. After it was sold, it went through two cycles of renovation in the middle of that decade, and again after changing hands in 1982. Both enhanced the site for leisure use by converting the premises to retail and restaurant facilities. The second phase introduced modernized shop fronts for greater visibility, large hand-made wooden signs, directory boards for wayfinding, banners and discerning neon lights, helping to contribute to an increase in retail sales by 50%. The square became an example for similar renovation projects across the world.

Visiting the square in recent times (50 years after the first renovation) reveals a building complex, still in good shape, but adorned by an assorted mix of old and new graphic elements on different scales. A permanent part of the complex is large white 'Ghirardelli' lettering (with illumination) scaffolded high above the square spanning the Cocoa and Mustard buildings and facing out towards the bay. This is the first identifier of the landmark you see on the approach along Beach Street. Each of the buildings, as they face out of the block, display a variation on the company name in ornate lettering, some dating the building and others merely naming it, such as the detailed 'CHOCOLATE BLD^C. Inside the square, the same graphic objects remain but as updated designs for directory boards and banners, and newer retail identities in neon.

Toilet signs carry not only the standardized symbols for men and women, but also include Braille; litter bins are colour coded, ATM machines branded, and steps painted with yellow warning stripes. Less permanent are the many bollards that restrict access to parts of the site or warn of hazards, and retailers display their wares in ways that stay in the memory (as well as in possession if purchased as gifts or mementos). Even cupcakes are decorated with a shamrock to induce sentiment for St Patrick's Day celebrations. In the tiniest details, we are reminded that Ghirardelli chocolate provides us with 'moments of timeless pleasure', when we drink from a mug purchased at the gift shop. All this serves to reinforce its status as a landmark, through graphic objects. See Plate 13.

La Défence, Hauts-de-Seine, France (1958–90 and to the present)

One of the unexpected benefits of visiting La Défence is looking back along the Avenue de la Grande Armee towards the centre of Paris. This affords an uninterrupted photogenic view through the Arc de Triomphe's void above the Tomb of the Unknown Soldier, providing a powerful sense of the axis that runs from the Louvre towards Versailles. When the Arc de Triomphe is looked at from the opposite direction – from the Place de la Concorde – it is not the case. Instead, the void of the Arc de Triomphe is cut in half by the top of La Grande Arche, La Défence's most recognizable building. This may seem trivial, but today the Arche is a major tourist attraction as well as a highly successful business district. Populated by many of the top 20 French corporations, estimates suggest there are as many as 180,000 employees, 25,000 residents, 45,000 students and 8 million tourists.

A long time in the planning, La Défence eventually took four decades to develop (the idea for a new business district can be traced back to the early twentieth century and the development of nodes on the Paris periphery to alleviate pressure on the city centre). The site's footprint occupies 2.9 square miles and connects to the centre of Paris via all of the main transportation routes. The view between the Arc de Triomphe and La Grande Arche is unrestricted due to the 40 hectare esplanade in front of the Arche, a pedestrian deck distinguished by open space, a geometric patterned surface, and an assortment of supersize and human size graphic elements. Large sculptures, directional signs, utility access points, advertising units, and retail displays provide a sparsely positioned patina of objects in and around the esplanade. Business, hotels, residential accommodation, the Quatre Temps shopping centre and an open-air museum featuring works by the likes of César and Alexander Calder provide the focus of activity.

Similar to much of Tokyo's new urban development, highlights of colour stand out from the 'grey' architecture and floorscape, the exception being the 'iconic' sculpture that lends its name to the complex, *La Défence de Paris* (1883) by Louis-Ernest Barrias.

Its life-like resemblance is matched by César Baldaccini's *Le Pouce* (1994), a larger-than-life sculpture of the artists thumb. By comparison, Calder's large *Red Spider* (1976) dwarfs other smaller colour highlights that define a basketball hoop or Metro entrance sign. See Plate 14.

Graphic objects at La Défence are dwarfed by the open space of the esplanade, but add a much-needed human dimension to the place, not least as a representation of interaction between people. These stand as isolated objects, yet fulfil to varying degrees all of the individual functions of graphic design, even in the way a refuse worker performs their duties in luminous attire.

Theater District and Times Square, New York (1967–74)

New York's Theater District, formed in 1967, evolved from wide-ranging zoning initiatives first introduced in 1961. As one of five 'special districts' – the others being the Lincoln Square Special Zoning District, the Fifth Avenue District, the Greenwich Street Special District in Lower Manhattan, and the Lower Manhattan Districts of Battery Park City and Manhattan Island – it originated from an emphasis on planning at the district level which, in turn, resulted in the formation of an Urban Design Group by then-mayor John Lindsay. The intention of that group, as noted by Lang (2005), was to 'stop the "haemorrhaging" of the city's life'. Broadway and its theatres were considered a high priority in this process, and the Times Square district benefited from further work by the Urban Design Group in the 1990s and 2000s.

Located at the northeast–southwest acute intersection of Broadway and Seventh Avenue, and connected to the east–west artery of 42nd Street, Times Square is at the heart of Manhattan's midtown Theater District. Some tourist guidebooks describe it as a 'top tourist attraction' for its innumerable monolithic advertising structures, comparable to other more familiar destinations such as the Statue of Liberty, Brooklyn Bridge, the Empire State Building, or Grand Central Station. Day and night, Times Square is an illuminated, dynamic display of graphic images sited on every available facade. Two of the most familiar views are the vertical stacks of display screens that demarcate the northeast and southwest edge of the 'square.'

One of the clearest views of Times Square is from the top of the amphitheatre-like steps at the northeast side, above the TKTS ticket booth. The incline directly faces the crucifix shaped 'Father Duffy' memorial with its inscription commemorating the work of Lt Colonel Duffy, pastor of the Holy Cross Church on 42nd Street. The sculpture, installed in 1937, is surrounded by contemporary static and dynamic images that adorn the fascias of buildings as a continuous frieze that defines the place and space.

Over the past three decades, far from light blight, the Times Square illuminations have contributed to making the area a safer place. As part of an attempt to upgrade the area, illuminated signs and their brightness levels have been regulated since 1987

(Boyer 2002), playing a considerable part in reducing crime incidents and significantly increasing real estate values in the area since the early 1990s. Enhanced by the formation of the Times Square Alliance in 1992 to improve and promote Times Square (also covering 40th Street to 53rd Street between 6th and 8th Avenues, and 46th Street between 8th and 9th Avenues) the place has experienced changing fortunes over recent decades. Some of this is attributed to the ever-changing and expanding presence of graphic objects in what has been called 'the world's most famous information environment' (Triggs 2009: 243)

However, the 'bright lights' of corporate advertising that encase Times Square are not the only graphic object on display. The New York Police Department (NYPD) signal their presence at the 43rd Street crossover with distinct neon lettering. This single-story station also carries a detailed external mosaic-tiled mural of the city's boroughs, as well as painted lettering reading 'Welcome to Times Square . . . NYPD'. NYPD uniformed officers are conspicuous in their distinctive blue uniform, and Times Square Alliance Public Safety Officers also have their own distinct regalia. The US Armed Forces seek to recruit from Times Square with the respective Army, Navy, Air Force and Marines circular crests exhibiting an invisible level of graphic detail in designs closely resembling the Presidential seal. Furthermore, the public can buy a copy of *USA Today* from a newsstand emblazoned with the newspaper's masthead, or theatre tickets from the booth located with the red TKTS totem protruding above head height.

More mundane are the numerous floor markings and manhole covers that speckle the floorscape (each belonging to different utility suppliers), and subway maintenance access denoted by a fluorescent yellow cover standing out from the grey floor. Furthermore, labelled garbage bins are part of an infrastructure that depends on 50 uniformed Times Square Alliance Sanitation Associates to do their work night and day. Retail premises display familiar and not-so-familiar fascia lettering and logotypes, whether the relatively sedate *Bravo Pizza* or brash *McDonald's* whose golden arches appear in multiple and different sizes to be seen close up and from afar. Some graphic objects are not fixed in the space such as a *TGI Fridays* hand-held sign that relies on human support positioned in view of oncoming pedestrians. In the same way advertising starts, stops and starts again, the traffic constantly streams through the artery-like streets, characterized by the consistent yellow livery of New York taxis. These physical manifestations represent Times Square as a densely populated array of graphic objects. See Plate 15.

Symbolic resources for changing livelihoods

All of the examples of urban graphic objects discussed throughout this book are symbolic representations, in more ways than are described by the semioticians' interpretation of a symbol. Putting a symbolic representation to good use in ways designed by someone for something for a transformative purpose has been called a 'symbolic resource' (Zittoun *et al.* 2003: 418). This captures the sentiment of much of what this book is about, if we read symbolic representation to mean graphic element. The interesting issue when framing our topic as a symbolic resource matter is the implication for things that contribute to emotional and identity formation through using things to achieve a specific purpose. A symbolic element, as described by Zittoun *et al.* (2003: 417) are 'shared concrete things, or some socially stabilized patterns of interaction or customs that encapsulate meanings or experiences for people' such as 'cultural artefacts, like books or films'. There is enough here to suggest that what we have been talking about throughout are symbolic resources, as these have an external and internal dimension. Externally, symbolic devices 'enable social interactions or concrete actions' whereas internally they 'regulate emotional experiences, change one's understanding of things or facilitate one's meaning constructions' (2003: 419). Using symbolic representations in this way as a symbolic resource is evident in many of the case studies discussed earlier. However, the following example is less conventional than those previously discussed, and demonstrates how the urban environment has been and continues to be a display space for homeless people in São Paulo.

The three previous case studies each benefit from the presence of graphic objects in how they have part-facilitated a change of use for old buildings (Ghirardelli Square), improve the attractiveness and connection between people, open space and buildings (LaDéfence), or help combat unsavoury activity and improve safety and security in an area (Times Square). Each of these are positive contributions to built environment concerns within professional urban design frameworks. However, it is not always the case that graphic objects are incorporated into what Carmona *et al.* (2010: 16–17) refer to as 'knowing' urban design – interventions may also happen because of 'unknowing' urban design. This essentially refers to the difference between people who consciously interpret their actions as doing urban design and those who do not acknowledge what they do as urban design. Our interpretation of this is that this latter group includes people who act on the city and impose a visual–aesthetic order on a place, no matter how incidental it may seem. We have not yet concentrated on the informality of graphic objects that sit outside more formal institutional contexts for design, such as graffiti or hand-generated graphic images of all kinds. However, there are plenty of instances where one might question the meanings associated with such images and places.

One such instance is in the Pinheiros area of São Paulo in the western part of the city – specifically a viaduct at the junction of Rue Galeno de Almeida and Rue João Moura. Underneath the viaduct is a graffiti-laden space where walls that line the street are covered in graffiti, concealing an enclave of waste recycling activity hidden behind (this being the reason the walls were built in the first place). Initially this was an underused and undeveloped space – what urban design has called a 'crack' in the urban core (Carmona *et al.* 2010: 11) – meaning a poor-quality space that has been overlooked in the development process. The space is now the location of the Co-operative of Autonomous Paper, Cardboard, Scraps and Reusable Materials Collectors

(COOPAMARE), the first organized co-operative of waste collectors in Brazil formed in 1989.

The co-operative was initially established in the early 1980s with the help of church workers who offered food and befriended homeless people who collected discarded waste from homes, industry and the retail trade, then sold them to raise funds to celebrate the Easter religious festival. Church workers started to hold meetings at a community centre in the Glicério neighbourhood of the city; this became an opportunity for collectors to meet regularly. Eventually a waste collectors' co-operative was formed under the guidance of the nuns. Called COOPAMARE, it was established by 20 collectors. Over time, it provided an income for members and the movement. It soon expanded to several cities across Brazil as COOPAMARE became a model for others to follow.

Initially, the viaduct land was used illegally, but now the city government has granted permission as a concession and the site has gradually been improved by the co-operative who have provided sanitation, electricity, running water, and restrooms. At the site, materials are sorted and recycled by co-operative workers engaging in a public environmental service for the community. Now, there are over 500 co-operatives with approximately 60,000 members across Brazil.

The space is dominated by an array of hand-painted images that communicate the identity of the co-operative and its association with the national movement of waste pickers, their respective identities writ large on the underpass support structures. The perimeter walls are adorned with highly sophisticated graffiti, which irritates the local residents in what is an affluent residential area.

Notices on the exterior of the co-operative advise on what kind of waste can be dropped off for sorting, as well as the its legal status and contact details. The co-operative workers wear their uniforms with the pride and dignity that comes with improved levels of self-esteem derived from their belief that they are providing a service to the community. Workers no longer see themselves as victims, but as citizens.

The church's formative role continues to be acknowledged and reflected in a fish drawn onto the adjacent road as a symbol of it's initial influence when establishing the co-operative and leading it to independence. See Plate 16.

Summary

This chapter has further exposed the duplicity of language when graphic objects are subjected to different disciplinary perspectives. Where one might expect some sense of stability, for example in the study of the image, there are overly simplified or overly complex classifications that provide some grounding, though the example of graphic images as *pictures, statues and designs* is not a cohesive triad. Similarly, discussion about representation introduced the notion of *language, signs and images* with little to commend it. From that, we explored the semiotic perspective on signs and although their interpretation of the word sign also has double meaning as a unity but also signifier and representamen, a triadic relationship between representaman, interpretant and referent provides one way to overcome sign confusion. This also avoids the semiotic of object as a thing to which a 'sign' is directed. Our purpose here has been to identify 'object' in the material sense, in the same way Kant defines it as an empirical object, or a representation in space, echoing our earlier discussion in Chapter 2 about graphic design as a spatial practice.

Furthermore, Peirce's three orders of sign as icon, index and symbol has been explained, but these do not exclusively apply to graphic objects. They may also stand for sound or gestures, symptoms or signals, and language in general. In essence, these characterize three types of representation from the literal to the abstract, each gradually being less associated with the thing to which the sign refers. An iconic sign resembles the thing it refers to; an indexical sign is more suggestive and associative, whereas a symbolic sign bares no relation at all in its form. Any meaning a symbolic sign has is purely by agreement between people. Within semiotics this is understood, but beyond there are other stronger associations with these words. For example, in graphic design, 'symbol' is most likely to imply a 'logo' of some kind (e.g Guinness uses a harp to represent the company) but in semiotic terms this most resembles an icon. Similarly, we have already reported on the reasons why the City of Westminster street nameplate is considered 'iconic', but the 'sign' does not bear any resemblance to a street! See Figure 6.2.

Finally, one of the more plausible explanations in this chapter about how we may structure our thinking about graphic objects comes from graphic design, and the individual functions of graphic design as information, persuasion, decoration, magic, metalinguistic and phatic. To establish what exactly graphic objects do we have

FIGURE 6.2 *Northumberland Avenue (London, 2009).*

Although considered an 'iconic' design, in semiotic terms the City of Westminster street nameplate is more symbolic than iconic because it has no resemblance to the thing it represents.

drawn from ideas about the function of graphic design in order to understand how graphic objects fulfil more than one purpose. This has been shown abundantly in case studies that reflect the smallest three of four types of urban design practice in Ghiraradelli Square in San Francisco, La Défence on the outskirts of Paris and in Times Square in Manhattan's Theater District. These highlight just how much graphic address facilitates the relationship between people and their environment. Furthermore, the idea of symbolic resources has been introduced and illustrated by focusing on graphic design as unknowing urban design. It appears that symbolic elements are utilized by both prosperous and less prosperous people in ways that transform their lives and surroundings.

7

Conclusion

'We now know that the art of city-making involves all the arts . . .'
LANDRY 2006: 5

This book has explored the relationship between graphic design and the urban environment through graphic objects as urban objects. It has worked towards this by referring various graphic forms back to their urban context in order to establish an understanding of different ensembles. The culmination has been the superimposition of graphic design on urban design work.

In order to explain the relationship between graphic objects and urban design, it has been necessary to first explain the argument from the perspective of graphic design and its potential as a spatial practice. This was initially considered by responding to the behest for an art and design perspective on what physically makes up or characterizes a city. Establishing such a perspective was shown to be difficult, if not impossible due to the heterogeneous nature of art and design and its prominence as an institutional administrative descriptor. Consequently, a graphic design stance evolved that took into account approaches to graphic communication beyond art and design, specifically geography and Lefebvre's notion representations of space, representational space and his concept of visual space. The culmination of this exploratory approach was framed as urban graphicacy. This advocates for fluency in the conceiving, planning and making of urban graphic communication through graphic design.

Having established the argument, it was further substantiated by defining an urban graphic object by putting it in an historical perspective. Chapter 3 revealed how graphic communication has been an integral and parallel part of human evolution and urban development since prehistoric times. Its systematic application emerged at the same times as cities became firmly established in Egypt, Mesopotamia, the Indus Valley and Central America. The urban context was revealed as having been significantly overlooked by graphic design historians, most probably due to the fact that it is a young academic discipline. Consequently, what discourse there is has failed to keep pace with the scale of urban development since the middle of the twentieth century. Two case studies illustrated how something as relatively insignificant as an inscription at the base of Trajan's Column in Rome provided the pattern for what is now London's letterform, used by millions of passengers on the city's transport infrastructure daily, and an integral but unacknowledged part of urban design work.

Chapters 4 and 5 took concepts from the urban design literature as their starting point. Lynch's concept of imageability, well-known in urban design but much less so in graphic design, depends in part on an urban-graphic analogy also used in the psychology, or micropsychology. This proved to be a key axis for this book and much of what we have done is to interrogate this on an urban scale. Concerns about language use also emerged in Chapter 4, particularly from the way Lynch wrote about signs with different meanings but without explanation. This duplicity is at the heart of a theory–practice divide in the field of graphic design. Instead, the macro–micro duality and the notion of mesographic analysis were introduced as a way to understand what was later explained as a 'syntagmatic' relationship (i.e. how meanings associated with graphic images are enhanced by their context). Two case studies from Shinjuku in Tokyo and the City of Westminster in London provided contrasting examples of how graphic objects define space. The first illustrated how an abundance of graphic objects in the Kabukichō area of Shinjuku merge into one big graphic object filling the urban landscape. Chapter 2 alluded to this relationship by defining the composite graphic object as a graphic space containing a set of graphic sub-objects. The second case study in Chapter 4 concentrated on the single systematic design of a street nameplate, which more simply demonstrated the notion of a composite graphic object comprising a graphic space, a set of graphic objects (typeface, rule, white rectangle and set of graphic relationships) within a single design. Both were shown to perform a unifying roll at the district level in the city image.

Whereas Lynch's ideas about imageability now date back more than half a century, Chapter 5 investigated more recent ways to frame image concerns as the visual dimension of urban design. The findings in this chapter revealed how graphic form is present in all dimensions of urban design, in particular how graphic objects might be framed within a pattern language. Once again, this pointed back to early work in the 1960s by Christopher Alexander and his explanation of form, context and ensemble, before a later discussion about pattern language. The form and context relationship as it appeared in the City of Westminster street nameplate and the Kabukichō area of Shinjuku were illustrated as diagrams which also helped to explain Alexander's ideas about fit and misfit, and how graphic design must purposely misfit to stand out. Even then, it must only serve a different set of contextual demands. Exemplifying this, the M of McDonald's and the M of Metro were seen to simply serve different causes. Notwithstanding the absence of graphic representation by Alexander *et al.* (1977) in *A Pattern Language,* 'road crossing' and 'ornamentation' were examined and reinterpreted for their graphic content.

Finally, Chapter 6 confronted the difficulties associated with the semiotic sign and whether all along we have or have not been appropriately referring to object as in graphic object. This chapter adopted *representamen* as its key theme on the basis that it is the form a sign takes. This connects to the earlier prompt about the form and context relationship in ensemble. Despite the many references to 'iconic' graphic designs in the literature that have emerged during the research for this book – the City of Westminster street nameplate, the Beatles *Abbey Road* album, or the *La Défence de Paris* statue – the semiotician's use of icon with index and symbol, is more deliberate, if more confusing in a cross-disciplinary sense. That said, we attempted to collapse the language of semiotics and reinstate object in the material sense, based on Kant's preference for the empirical object. Lastly, the individual functions of graphic objects laid the foundation for identifying the purpose of graphic objects in urban objects. This guided the examination of graphic objects in three urban design case studies and much less formal examples of design in the urban environment.

Ultimately, this book has shown how inadequately graphic objects are understood in the built environment and has provided some historical and theoretical context to change this situation. The trans-disciplinary nature of the references that inform the research will expose the content to criticism for a lack of depth at times, and this is entirely expected. If looked at from a graphic design perspective (the stance from which this book is written) this does not hold true. The empirical evidence of the various scenarios, object and environmental case studies reveal how the products of graphic design appear both in urban objects and as urban objects across the full range of urban design practice.

Bibliography

Alexander, C. (1964). *Notes on the Synthesis of Form*, Cambridge MA and London: Harvard University Press.

Alexander, C., Ishikawa, S., Silverstein, M., Jacobson, M., Fiksdahl-King, I., and Angel, S. (1977). *A Pattern Language: towns, buildings, construction*, New York: Oxford University Press.

Anon. (1950). 'Bus-stopping'. *Design*(22), 32.

Anon. (1997). *The Zebra, Pelican and Puffin Pedestrian Crossings Regulations and General Directions 1997*, London: The Stationery Office.

Anon. (1999). 'La peinture après l abstraction 1955–1975'. City: Paris-Musées.

Anon. (2004). *Research Notes: The new definition of urban and rural areas of England and Wales*, The Countryside Agency. Available at: www.publications.naturalengland.org.uk/file/86018.

Anon. (2013). *The Rural–Urban Classification for England*, Government Statistical Service. Available at: www.gov.uk/government/uploads/system/uploads/attachment_data/file/248666/Rural-Urban_Classification_leaflet__Sept_2013_.pdf.

Archer, C., and Parré, A. (2005). *Paris Underground*, West New York: Mark Batty Publisher.

Arthur, P., and Passini, R. (1992). *Wayfinding: People, Signs and Architecture*, Toronto: McGraw-Hill Ryerson.

Arthur, P., and Passini, R. ([1992] 2002). *People, Signs and Architecture*, Toronto: McGraw-Hill Ryerson.

Ascher, K. (2005). *The Works: Anatomy of a City*, London: Penguin Books Ltd.

Ascher, K. ([2005] 2007). *Works: Anatomy of a City*, New York: Penguin Books.

Aslam, A., and Szczuka, J. (2012). *The State of the World's Children 2012: Children in an Urban World*, United Nations Children's Fund (UNICEF). New York. Available at: www.unicef.org/sowc2012/.

Ausubel, J. H., and Herman, R. (1988). 'Cities and their Vital Systems', *Series on Technology and Social Priorities*. Washington DC: National Academy Press.

Baeder, J. (1996). *Sign Language: street signs as folk art*, New York: Harry N Abrams.

Baines, P., and Dixon, C. (2002). 'Exploiting context', in D. Jury, (ed.), *Typographic 59*.

Baines, P., and Dixon, C. (2003). *Signs: lettering in the environment*, London: Lawrence King.

Baines, P., and Dixon, C. (2004). 'Letter rich Lisbon'. *Eye Magazine*, 14(54).

Baines, P., and Dixon, C. (2005). '*Sense of Place*'. *Eye Magazine*. London: Haymark Busines Publications 58–64.

Baines, P., and Haslam, A. (2005). *Type and Typography*, London: Lawrence King Publishing Ltd.

Barilli, R. (1969). *Art Nouveau*, R. Rudorff, trans., Feltham: The Hamlyn Publishing Group Limited.

Barnard, M. (2005). *Graphic Design as Communication*, London: Routledge.

Barthes, R. ([1957] 2009). *Mythologies*, A. Lavers, trans., London: Vintage.

Bartram, A. (1975). *Lettering in Architecture*, London: Lund Humpries.

Bartram, A. (1978a). *Fascia Lettering in the British Isles*, London: Lund Humpries.

Bartram, A. (1978b). *Street Name Lettering in the British Isles*, London: Lund Humphries.

Berger, C. M. (2005). *Wayfinding: designing and implementing graphic navigational systems*, Mies: Rotovision SA.

Bertin, J. ([1967] 1983). *Semiology of Graphics*, W. J. Berg, trans., Madison: University of Wisconsin Press.

Blackburn, S. (1999). *Think*, Oxford: Oxford University Press.

Blumer, H. (1969). *Symbolic Interactionism: Perspective and Method,* California: University of California Press.

Boardman, D. (1983). *Graphicacy and Geography Teaching*, Beckenham: Croom Helm Ltd.

Bowallius, M.-L. (2002). 'Tradition and Innovation in Swedish Graphic Design 1910–1950', in C. Widenheim, (ed.), *Utopia and Reality: Modernity in Sweden 1900–1960*. New Haven and London: Yale University Press.

Boyer, M. C. (2002). 'Twice-told Stories: The Double Erasure of Times Square', in I. Borden, J. Kerr, J. Rendell, and A. Pivaro, (eds), *The Unknown City: contesting architecture and social space.* Cambridge, MA: The MIT Press, 30–53.

Brockmann, J. M. (1995). *Pioneer of Swiss Graphic Design*, Baden: Lars Müller Publishers.

Buchler, J. (1955). 'Philosophical Writings of Peirce', New York: Dover Publications, Inc.

Bullivant, L. (2006). *Responsive Environments*, London: V&A Publications.

Burke, G. (1976). *Townscape*, Harmondsworth: Pelican Books.

CABE. (2001). *The Value of Urban Design*, Tonbridge: Thomas Telford.

CABE. (2002). *Paving the Way: how we achieve clean, safe and attractive streets*, Tonbridge: Thomas Telford.

Calvino, I. ([1972] 1997). *Invisible Cities*, London: Vintage.

Carmona, M., Heath, T., Oc, T., and Tiesdell, S. (2003). *Public Places – Urban Spaces: the dimensions of urban design*, Oxford: Architectural Press.

Carmona, M., Heath, T., Oc, T., and Tiesdell, S. (2010). *Public Places – Urban Spaces: the dimensions of urban design*, Oxford: Architectural Press.

Carr, S. (1973). *City Signs and Lights: A Policy Study*, Cambridge MA: The MIT Press.

Carrington, N. (1951). 'Legibility or "Architectural Appropriateness"'. *Design*(32), 27–9.

Carrington, N., and Harris, M. (1951). 'The British Contribution to Industrial Art.' *Design*(31), 2–7.

Chandler, D. (2007). *Semiotics: the basics*, New York: Routledge.

CNAA (1990). *Vision and Change: a review of graphic design studies in polytechnics and colleges*, London: Council for National Academic Awards.

Cohen, D., and Anderson, S. (2006). *A Visual Language: elements of design*, London: The Herbert Press.

Coulston, J. C. (1988). *Trajan's Column: the sculpting and relief content of a Roman propaganda monument*, Newcastle: The University of Newcastle upon Tyne.

Cowan, R. (1997). *The Connected City: A new approach to making cities work*. London: Urban Initiatives.

Cramsie, P. (2010). *The Story of Graphic Design*, London: The British Library.

Cullen, G. (1971). *The Concise Townscape*, London: The Architectural Press.

Davies, P., and Wagner, C. (2000). *Streets for All: a guide to the management of London's streets*. London: English Heritage.

Davis, M. (2012). *Graphic Design Theory*, London: Thames & Hudson Ltd.

de Saussure, F. (1915). *Course in General Linguistics*, London: McGraw-Hill Books Company.

Del Genio, C. I., Gross, T., and Bassler, K. E. (2011). Graphicality Transitions in Scale-free Networks. Available at: http://cds.cern.ch/record/1362125.

Dorst, K. (2003). *Understanding Design*, Amsterdam: BIS Publishers.

Drucker, J., and McVarish, E. (2013). *Graphic Design History: a critical guide*, London: Pearson.

Dwiggins, D. A. ([1922] 1999). 'New kind of printing calls for new design', in M. Bierut, J. Helfland, S. Heller, and R. Poyner, (eds), *Looking Closer 3*. New York: Allworth Press, 14–18.

Eaves, M. (2002). 'Graphicality: multimedia fables for "textual" critics', in E. Bergmann Loizeaux and N. Fraistat, (eds), *Reimagining Textuality: textual studies in the late age of print*. Madison, WI: University of Wisconsin Press.

Elkins, J. (1999). *The Domain of Images*, New York: Cornell University Press.

Eskilson, S. J. (2012). *Graphic Design: a history*, London: Lawrence King.

Fella, E. (2000). *Letters on America: photographs and lettering*, London: Laurence King.

Friedman, K. (1998). 'Building Cyberspace. Information, Place and Policy', *Built Environment*, 24(2/3), 83–103.

Friend, L., and Hefter, J. (1935). *Graphic Design: A Library of Old and New Masters in the Graphic Arts*, New York and London: Whittley House, McGraw-Hill Book Co.

Fuller, S. M. (1843). *Summer on the Lakes, in 1843*, Boston: Little Brown.

Garfield, S. (2010). *Just my Type*, London: Profile Books.

Ghosh, P. (2014). 'Cave paintings change ideas about the origin of art'. BBC News. Available at: www.bbc.co.uk/news/science-environment-29415716.

Gray, N. (1960). *Lettering on Buildings*, London: The Architectural Press.

Hall, S. (1997). *Representation: cultural representations and signifying practices*, London: SAGE 400.

Harland, R. G. (2012). 'Towards an Integrated Pedagogy of Graphics in the United Kingdom', *Iridescent, Icograda Journal of Design Research*, 2(1).

Harland, R. G. (2015a). 'Graphic Objects and their Contribution to the Image of the City', *Journal of Urban Design*, Volume and Issue tbc. (in press).

Harland, R. G. (2015b). 'Seeking to build graphic theory from graphic design research', in P. A. Rodgers and J. Yee, (eds), *The Routledge Companion to Design Research*, London and New York: Routledge 87–97.

Hawking, S., and Mlodinow, L. (2010). *The Grand Design*, London: Bantam Press.

Heathcote, D. (1999). 'Big Book, Little Buildings', *Eye Magazine*, London: Quantum Publishing.

Helfland, J. (2001). *Screen: essays on graphic design, new media, and visual culture*, New York: Princeton Architectural Press.

Heller, S. (1999). M. Bierut, J. Helfland, S. Heller, and R. Poyner, (eds), *Looking Closer 3*. New York: Allworth Press.

Heller, S., and Vienne, V. (2012). *100 Ideas that Changed Graphic Design*, London: Laurence King Publishing.

Hollis, R. (2001). *Graphic Design: a concise history*, London: Thames and Hudson Ltd.

Johnston, E. ([1906] 1977). *Writing & Illuminating & Lettering*, London: A & C Black.

Jubert, R. ([2005] 2006). *Tyopgraphy and Graphic Design: from Antiquity to the Present*, D. Radzinowicz and D. Dusinberre, trans., Paris: Flammarion.

Kant, I. (2007 [1781]). *Critique of Pure Reason*, W. Marcus, trans. London: Penguin Books Ltd.

Kepes, G. (1944). *Language of Vision*: Wisconsin IN: The Wisconsin Cuneo Press.

Kinneir, J. (1980). *Words and Buildings: the art and practice of public lettering*, London: The Architectural Press.

Landry, C. (2006). *The Art of City Making*, London: Earthscan.

Lang, J. (1994). *Urban Design: the American experience*, New York: John Wiley & Sons, Inc.

Lang, J. (2005). *Urban design: a typology of procedures and products*, Oxford: Architectural Press.

Lefebvre, H. (1970). *The Urban Revolution/Henri Lefebvre*; trans. Robert Bononno, Minneapolis: The University of Minnesota Press.

Lefebvre, H. (1991). *The Production of Space/Henri Lefebvre*; trans. Donald Nicholson Smith, Oxford: Blackwell Publishing.

Lefebvre, H. (1996). *Writings on Cities/Henri Lefebvre; selected, translated, and introduced by Eleonore Kofman and Elizabeth Lebas*, Oxford: Blackwell Publishing.

LeGates, R. T. (2003). 'How to Study Cities', in R. T. LeGates and F. Stout, (eds), *The City Reader*, London and New York: Routledge.

LeGates, R. T., and Stout, F. (2003). *The City Reader*, Routledge: London and New York.

Lethaby, W. R. ([1906] 1977). *Editor's Preface, Writing & Illuminating & Lettering*, by Edward Johnston. London: A & C Black.

Lewis, J., and Brinkley, J. (1954). *Graphic Design*, London: Routledge & Kegan Paul.

Leyens, J.-P., Yzerbyt, V., and Schadron, G. (1994). *Stereotypes and Social Cognition*, London: SAGE.

Livingston, A., and Livingston, I. (1992). *The Thames and Hudson Dictionary of Graphic Design and Designers*, London: Thames and Hudson Ltd.

Lovegrove, K. (2003). *Graphicswallah: graphics in India*, London: Lawrence King.

Lucas, G. (2011). 'Heard the one about the artist, the designer and the carpet of concrete', *Creative Review*, London: Centaur Communications Limited. London.

Lucas, G. (2013). 'A most distinctive corporate typeface', *Creative Review*, London: Centaur Media 26–30.

Lupton, E. (1996). *Mixing Messages: graphic design in contemporary culture*, New York: Princeton Architectural Press.

Lussu, G. (2001). 'Adventure on the Undergroud', in D. Jury, (ed.), *TypoGraphic Writing*. ISTD.

Lynch, K. (1960). *The Image of the City*, Cambridge, MA and London: The MIT Press.

Lynch, K. (1981). *Good City Form*, Cambridge, MA and London: The MIT Press.

Manghani, S., Arthur, P., and Simons, J. (2006). *Images: a reader*, London: SAGE Publications Ltd.

Marshall, G. (1998). *A Dictionary of Sociology*, Oxford: Oxford University Press.

McDermott, C. (2007). *Design: the key concepts*, Oxford: Routledge.

Meggs, P. B. (1983). *A History of Graphic Design*, London: Allen Lane.

Meggs, P., and Purvis, A. W. (2006). *Meggs' History of Graphic Design*, Chichester: John Wiley & Sons.

Meggs, P. B. (2014). 'Graphic Design'. Available at: www.britannica.com/EBchecked/topic/1032864/graphic-design.

Middendorp, J. (2008). 'Amsterdam bridge lettering', in D. Quay, (ed.), *Typographic 67*, Taunton: International Society of Typographic Designers.

Miller, J. (1999). *Nowhere in Particular*, London: Mitchell Beazley.

Mirzoeff, N. (2013). *The Visual Culture Reader*, Oxford: Routledge.

Mitchell, W. J. T. (1986). *Iconology: image, text, ideology*, Chicago: The University of Chicago Press.

Moles, A. M. (1989). 'The legibility of the world: a project of graphic design', in V. Margolin, (ed.), *Design discourse: history, theory, criticism*, Chicago: The University of Chicago Press, 119–29.

Mollerup, P. (2005). *Wayshowing*, Baden: Lars Müller Publishers.

Monmonier, M. (1993). *Mapping It Out: Expository Cartography for the Humanities and Social Sciences*, Chicago: University of Chicago Press, 4–12.

Mumford, L. ([1937] 2003). 'What is a City?', in R. T. LeGates and F. Stout, (eds), *The City Reader*, London and New York: Routledge.

Needham, B. (1977). *How Cities Work*, Oxford: Pergamon Press.

Nelson, H. G., and Stolterman, E. (2012). *The Design Way: intentional change in an unpredictable world*, Cambridge and London: The MIT Press.

Newark, Q. (2002). *What is Graphic Design?*, London: RotoVision SA.

O'Pray, I. (2013). 'Fake zebra crossing is painted on busy street', Harborough Mail 3. Available at: www.harboroughmail.co.uk/news/mail-news/fake-zebra-crossing-is-painted-on-busy-street-1-5279771.

Perkins, C. (2003). 'Cartography and graphicacy', in N. J. Clifford, S. L. Holloway, S. P. Rice, and G. Valentine, (eds), *Key Methods in Geography*, London: SAGE, 343–368.

Perkins, T. (2000). 'The Geometry of Roman Lettering', *Font: Sumner Stone, Calligraphy and Type Design in a Digital Age*, Ditchling, Sussex: Edward Johnston Foundation and Ditchling Museum.

Poe, E. A. (1858). *The Works of the Late Edgar Allan Poe: with a memoir by R. W. Griswold and notices of his life and genius by N. P. Willis and J. R. Lowell. Vol. III, the literati. New York: Redfield*, New York: Redfield.

Poetter, R. S. (1908). 'Graphic Design for reinforcing Rectangular Concrete Sections', *Cement Age*, VI(2), 226–32.

Poyner, R. (1999). 'Typographica: modernism and eclecticism', *Eye Magazine*, 8(31), 64–73.

Poyner, R. (2002). *Typographica*, New York: Princeton Architectural Press.

Poyner, R. (2003). *No More Rules: graphic design and postmodernism*, London: Laurence King Publishing.

Pylyshyn, Z. W. (2007). *Things and places : how the mind connects with the world*, Cambridge MA and London: The MIT Press.

QAA. (2008). *Subject Benchmark Statements: art and design*, Gloucester: The Quality Assurance Agency for Higher Education.

Queiroz, J., and Farias, P. A. (2014). 'On Peirce's Visualization of the Classification of Signs: Finding a Common Pattern in Diagrams', in Thellefsen, T. Sorensen, and Bent, (eds), *Charles Sanders Peirce in His Own Words – 100 Years of Semiotics, Communication and Cognition*, Berlin: Walter de Grouyer, 283–90.

Rowe, C., and Koetter, F. (1978). *Collage City*, Cambridge, MA, and London: The MIT Press.

Roylance, B., Quance, J., Craske, O., and Milisic, R. (2000). 'The Beatles Anthology', London: Cassell & Co.

Rykwert, J. (1988). *The Idea of a Town*, Cambridge, MA: MIT Press.

Scollon, R., and Wong Scollon, S. (2003). *Discourses in Place: Language in the Material World*, London: Routledge.

Seago, A. (n.d.). 'ARK Magazine: the Royal College of Art and Postmodernism', in C. Frayling and C. Catterall, (eds), *Design of the Times: one hundred years of the Royal College of Art*, Shepton Beauchamp: Richard Dennis.

Shaw, P. (2014). '*Graphic Design': A brief terminological history*. Available at: www.paulshawletterdesign.com/2014/06/graphic-design-a-brief-terminological-history/.

Shimojima, A. (1999). 'The Graphic-Linguistic Distinction: Exploring Alternatives.' *Artificial Intelligence Review*, 13(4), 313–35.

Simon, H. A. (1996). *The Sciences of the Artificial*, Cambridge, MA: The MIT Press.

Soanes, C., and Stevenson, A. (2005). *Oxford Dictionary of English*, Oxford: Oxford University Press.

Soar, M. (2004). 'Excoffon's autograph', *Eye Magazine*, 14(54), 50–7.

Soja, E., W. (2010). *Seeking Spatial Justice*, Minneapolis: University of Minnesota Press.

Steel, C. (2009). *Hungry City: how food shapes our lives*, London: Vintage Books.

Stöckl, H. (2005). 'Typography: body and dress of a text – a signing mode between language and image', *Visual Communication*, 4(2), 204–14.

Strauss, A. L. (1961). *Images of the American City*, New York: The Free Press of Glencoe.

Sutton, J. (1965). *Signs in Action*, London: Studio Vista.

Thaler, R. H., and Keller, D. ([2008] 2009). *Nudge*, London: Penguin Books

Thrift, N. (2009). 'Space: the fundamental stuff of geography', in N. J. Clifford, S. L. Holloway, S. P. Rice, and G. Valentine, (eds), *Key Methods in Geography*, London: SAGE, 85–96.

Tillman, T. (1990). *The Writings on the Wall: peace at the Berlin Wall*, Santa Monica: 22/7 publishing company.

Tomrley, C. G. (1950). 'Official lettering gives a lead', *Design*(14), 12–14.

Tonkiss, F. (2013). *Cities by Design: the social life of urban form*, Cambridge: Polity Press.

Triggs, T. (2009). 'Editorial', *Visual Communication*, 8(3), 243–7.

Tschichold, J. ([1928] 1998). *The New Typography: A Handbook for Modern Designers*, trans. Ruari McLean, Berkeley: University of California Press.

Twyman, M. (1982). 'The graphic presentation of language,' *Information Design Journal*, 3(1), 2–22.

UN-Habitat. (2008). *State of World Cities 2008/2009: Harmonious Cities*, London: Earthscan.

van der Waarde, K. (2009). *On graphic design: listening to the reader*: Avans Hogeschool Research Group Visual Rhetoric AKV St. Joost.

Venturi, R., Scott Brown, D., and Izenour, S. (1977). *Learning from Las Vegas*, Cambridge MA, and London: The MIT Press.

von Engelhardt, J. (2002). *The Language of Graphics: A framework for the analysis of syntax and meaning in maps, charts and diagram*, University of Amsterdam, Institute for Logic, Language and Computation.

Walker, J. A. (1995). 'The London Underground diagram', in T. Triggs, (ed.), *Communicating Design: essays in visual communication*, London: B.T. Batsford Ltd.

Ward, L. F. (1902). 'Contemporary Sociology', *American Journal of Sociology*, 7(5), 629–58.

Waugh, D. (2000). *Geography: an integrated approach*, Walton-on-Thames: Nelson.

White, R. M. (1988). 'Preface', in J. H. Ausubel and R. Herman, (eds), *Cities and their Vital Systems*, Washington DC: National Academy Press.

Williams, G. (1954). 'Street Furniture', *Design*(69), 15–33.

Wilmot, P. D. (1999). 'Graphicacy as a form of communication', *South African Geographical Journal*, 81(2), 91–5.

Zittoun, T., Duveen, G., Gillespie, A., Ivinson, G., and Psaltis, C. (2003). 'The Use of Symbilic Resources in Development Transitions', *Culture & Psychology*, 9(4), 415–48.

Index

Numbers in italics denote tables and numbers in bold denote photographs and diagrams